Thunder Cloud
– Managing Reward in a Digital Age

Daniel Hibbert

About the author

Daniel Hibbert has over 20 years of experience in advising businesses on reward and performance. For most of this time he has worked with global professional services firms and now works as an independent consultant. He is a Fellow of the Chartered Institute of Personnel and Development and previously qualified as an accountant and tax advisor.

Daniel lives in Bedfordshire, England with his wife and two children.

Acknowledgements

I would like to thank the clients and colleagues who have taught me everything I have learnt over the years, and without whom this book could not have been written. I would also like to thank Jacquie Findlay for her helpful comments and suggestions on the draft manuscript. Any remaining errors are entirely my responsibility.

Dedication

To Penny, Thomas and Alice

Contents

Table of figures

Introduction

Reward poses a predicament for many employers: how can **pay** be managed to motivate employees and simultaneously provide value for money for the business? Usually the response is to leave it alone and carry on with what has been done in the past, taking refuge in so-called "best practice". This response is becoming untenable in a rapidly changing digital age.

Pay is a significant cost for businesses and it is the most important part of reward for most employees. It is also the part of reward that gets the least management attention. Most expertise is directed at managing pensions, benefits, share incentives and executive remuneration. Pay is not as technically complex as these other areas of reward, but it is crucial to the **employment relationship**. The management of pay is difficult and employers tend to look for solutions in market data and in **job evaluation** processes. They usually play it safe and continue with the established practices that they have been using for many years.

Do these approaches still work for organisations in the digital age? The world of work has changed dramatically in the past fifty years. The jobs that most people do have become more complex, varied and changeable. Often the skills and experience that individuals bring to their work makes a big difference to the outcomes from the job. Modern thinking as to what motivates employees, and especially the importance of autonomy and intrinsic motivation, gives employers the opportunity to re-think the way they manage people.

The philosopher Karl Popper used the metaphor of clouds and clocks[1]. Clocks are mechanical devices and it is easy to predict what they might do in the future. Clouds are part of a vast, complex ecosystem and it is very difficult to predict how they will behave. Some big mistakes in life come from trying to manage clouds as if they were clocks. This is why so many large and complex projects go wrong, opinion polls cannot be relied on, and the setting of targets often produces perverse outcomes. Anything that involves human behaviour is more like a cloud than a clock.

Reward is usually treated as if it were a clock but it is definitely a cloud. The way people respond to it is unpredictable and often irrational; small changes can have large effects and sometimes big changes have very little impact. It is like a thunder cloud that builds up on a hot summer afternoon. It might produce some heavy rain, sleet or snow, or bright sunshine might suddenly emerge as the cloud moves away and a rainbow might be seen.

As we move into the new digital age, the thunder cloud of reward has become darker and less predictable. The nature of employment is changing and the psychological aspects of the employment relationship have become more important. Information is more readily available and travels faster than ever before. The jobs that people are doing are also very different: they are more knowledge-based, complicated and self-managed. Many employers are using reward practices that were designed for the simpler style of jobs that people were doing fifty years ago.

There is much confusion about the meaning of the word "reward", as there is with much of the language that is used in the world of Human Resources (HR). In this book, reward consists of pay (salary and bonuses), pension, benefits, share incentives, and other **extrinsic rewards**. It also includes the psychological or **intrinsic rewards**, which are a vital part of employment relationships in the digital age. I have tried to adopt a clear and consistent language in the way key words are used. At the end of the book, there is a list of Definitions and defined terms are in bold print where they first appear.

Part 1 explains how reward is managed, shows how developments in social sciences bring fresh thinking, and describes some of the things in reward management that do not work. Part 2 outlines a new way of thinking about reward, and then goes on to suggest some new ways of approaching **pay framework** design, performance-related pay and how reward should be managed. The book draws on developments in behavioural science, including motivation theory and behavioural economics, to show how this knowledge is so valuable in the management of reward. It also draws heavily on my twenty years of experience in helping organisations with their reward issues. I owe much to the clients and colleagues who have given me so many insights over this time.

You will notice (if you manage to get beyond the second chapter of this book!) that I am not a great admirer of the finance profession. This is nothing personal - I like accountants and have spent much of my career working for accounting firms. I qualified as an accountant and abandoned the number counting profession about twenty-five years ago when I realised that people are so much more interesting than numbers. There is a fetish in the business world with trying to measure everything, which leads to the very dangerous assumption that once something is measured it is understood. Finance people are particularly susceptible to this because of the training they have had. Organisations would often be better managed if the accountants stuck to their job of looking after the numbers and allowed those responsible for talent management to look after reward.

What is the role of reward in making our organisations more effective? How can reward be used to engage with the workforce? What are the pitfalls in getting it wrong? Does reward matter or is it best left alone? This book gives a framework for thinking about reward and provides some answers to these questions. It does not provide solutions because there are no right or wrong answers, and each employer needs to develop the approach that best fits with what they need to achieve. It does provide ideas for a new way of thinking about reward, showing how it can make a positive contribution to the management of people in the digital age.

Part 1 – The need for change

Chapter 1. The basics

What the Romans did for us

The idea of pay developed as civilisations became more sophisticated. Slaves gave their labour in exchange for food and shelter and free citizens were able to exchange money for their labour. As institutions needed to deploy larger numbers of people, pay structures began to be used for the first time. Figure 1 explains the pay structure that operated in the Roman army[2]:

Figure 1. **Roman army payscales**

Payscales for different grades of Roman soldier in Auxiliary units
Cohors - Infantry units   *Ala* - Cavalry units

PAY SCALE (X basic pay)	COHORS RANK (infantry) in ascending order	AMOUNT (denarii)	ALA RANK (cavalry) (in ascending order)	Amount (denarii)
1 X *caligati* – 'rankers'	**Pedes** infantryman	188	**Gregalis** ala cavalryman	263
1.5 X *sesquiplicarii* 'one-and-half-pay men'	**Tesserarius** corporal	282	**Sesquiplicarius** corporal	395
2 X *duplicarii* 'double-pay men'	**Signifer** centuria standard-bearer **Optio** centurion's deputy **Vexillarius** cohort standard-bearer	376	**Signifer** turma standard-bearer **Curator** decurion's deputy **Vexillarius** ala standard-bearer	526
Over 5 X	**Centurio**(n) centuria commander **Centurio princeps** chief centurion **Beneficiarius** deputy cohort commander	940 +	**Decurio** benefici = turma commander **Decurio princeps** chief benefici **Beneficiarius** deputy ala commander	1,315 +
50 X	**Praefectus** or **Tribunus** cohort commander	9,400	**Praefectus** or **Tribunus** (ala commander)	13,150

Infantry *Cohors* were divided into *centuria* (centuries) of 80 men under the leadership of a *Centurio* (Centurion)
Cavalry *Ala* were divided into *turma* of 60 men and their horses under the leadership of a *Decurio* (Decurion)

It is two thousand years old, yet remains similar to many of the pay structures that are still used today. It is based on rank. There are different levels of pay for the different ranks and different amounts for cavalry and infantry. It is open and transparent. Therefore, it is easy to understand how the structure fits together and to see what is paid for the different roles. A judgement could be made as to whether the system is fair, based on an understanding of the jobs and this simple table. This type of structure was used for the military and other government organisations for many years before the Industrial Revolution.

With the Industrial Revolution, organisations got bigger and more complex, but most jobs remained simple with clear and pre-prescribed tasks. Pay was based on the hierarchy, with tightly defined jobs, and it was easy to be transparent about the pay structure. Employees usually knew what others were paid and could see what they might be paid if they were promoted upwards through the hierarchy.

In the 20th century, Trade Unions became more effective in obtaining improvements to working conditions and in getting pay increases for the (almost entirely male) groups of workers they represented. Trade Unions were, and still are, supportive of open and transparent Roman army-type pay structures. However, as terms and conditions improved, employers began to provide a greater range of benefits, including pensions and paid holidays.

It was only towards the end of the last century that the occupational segregation between jobs commonly carried out by men and women began to break down. In 1970, The Equal Pay Act was introduced in the UK to make it unlawful to pay differently if work carried out by men and women was assessed as being of equal value. Sophisticated job evaluation systems were developed to assess the value of work, and they were used to underpin pay structures. The underlying structures did not change, but they became more difficult to manage as jobs became more complex and varied.

There are two problems with the Roman army pay structure. The first of these is that where there are skills shortages it might be necessary to pay more than the amount indicated by the internal structures to recruit and retain employees with the requisite skills. The rigid structure based on internal equity does not readily enable this to be done. Nonetheless, in a competitive and flexible labour market, this approach is increasingly important to businesses.

The second problem is how to reward **performance**, and individual performance in particular. Where several employees are carrying out the same job there are often differences in individual performance and contribution. Traditional pay structures do not recognise these differences. As jobs become increasingly complex in the digital age, differences in individual contribution have a large impact.

The simplicity and transparency of the Roman army pay system is unworkable in the modern world. The challenge is try to replace it with something with similar coherence and simplicity. To address these issues many employers have abandoned rigid structures and manage their pay systems based on a combination of **market rate** and performance.

Criteria for pay decisions

Employers base their pay decisions on the three criteria shown below:

Figure 2.   Criteria for pay decisions

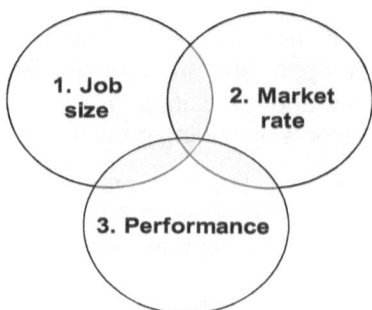

1. **Job size** refers to the size of the job and the internal equity that applies within the organisation. Job size is assessed through job evaluation or levelling systems that "size" the job, using yardsticks such as the level of responsibilities, knowledge and skills that can be applied on the same basis to all jobs in the organisation. The size of the job is usually the basis for ensuring that pay is equitable within the organisation.

2. **Market rate** is the amount that is typically paid by other employers for the same job. It is therefore the amount that needs to be paid to ensure that pay is competitive with the external market.

3. **Performance** is the amount that is paid for performance, which may be organisational, team, or individual performance. Performance can be used to determine the level of base salary, bonus, or a combination of these.

Different employers place different emphasis on each of the three criteria, and few are explicit about how they use them. In the public sector, internal equity and transparency are important and much of the emphasis is on job size. In the private sector, market rate and performance are more important.

Reward strategy

The framework for making reward decisions should be guided by the organisation's **reward strategy**. The reward strategy may place more emphasis on one of the three criteria over others, but all three should be an integral part of reward decisions. For example, organisations that rely solely on job evaluation to determine pay will often still apply market supplements for jobs where there is a scarcity of skills. Even in situations where performance does not form part of the reward strategy, business performance will still be a part of the consideration in determining the amount of annual pay increases.

The reward strategy should give the employer the policies and processes it needs to enable rational reward decisions to made, striking the right balance between job size, market rate and performance.

It is essential that pay decisions are seen to be fair, but this does not mean that they also have to be objective. Fairness and objectivity are not useful words in the management of reward – everyone agrees that they are important and necessary, but the words mean very different things to different people. This book prefers to use the word "rational" when describing pay decisions, which means "based on, or in accordance with, reason or logic"[3]. Pay can be rational without being objective if the subjectivity is exercised rationally.

To enable rational pay decisions to be made employers adopt reward strategies, which usually include the organisation's policies on:

- How jobs are evaluated and placed into grades,
- The positioning of reward with the external market, and
- The approach to linking pay with performance.

These strategies are often developed for the stated purpose of being open and transparent to enable employees and others to see how pay is determined. In practice most reward strategies are rather bland, and do not convey meaningful information. The criteria for making pay decisions, and some of the difficulties with these, are discussed further in Chapter 3. The following parts of this chapter give some more detail on how each component of reward operates.

Pay

Pay, which usually takes the form of base salary and bonuses, is the most important part of reward. Base salary is important, not just because it is the largest component of reward, but it is also the number that can most easily be compared with other organisations. It is usually what attracts employees to the organisation and is most likely to cause them to leave if they could earn more elsewhere.

Bonuses are the amounts paid in addition to base salary. The amounts paid often vary with the performance of the employer. When the company has a good year, higher bonuses are paid, and when things are not going so well the amounts paid reduce.

Bonuses can also be based on individual or team performance, and many bonus plans combine this with company performance. One of the problems with bonus scheme design is that they are too complicated, often based on a combination of all of these things. This issue is discussed further in Chapter 6.

Pensions

As organisations became more sophisticated, company pension plans became widespread so that employers could provide for their employees in retirement. Employers wanted to be sure that their employees were provided for when their working lives were over, and the promise to do this became an important part of the reward package they offered to employees.

As life expectancy increased throughout the last century, pensions became a more valuable part of reward, especially while the retirement age for most people was around sixty. As the population aged, and for a long time the retirement age was unchanged, pensions became less affordable for employers. The old model of providing a defined benefit pension, based on the salary at the end of the employment, is now largely obsolete. In the UK public sector, pensions have moved to being based on career average earnings and most private sector pension plans are based on the defined contribution model, with the risk on investment returns being transferred to the employee.

Pensions still seem to get more attention than any other part of reward. This is because they are complex and the uncertainties relating to the future costs of defined benefit schemes mean that they can have a significant impact on costs for the employer. A whole industry has developed to advise organisations on the management of their pension schemes. Unfortunately, pensions are rarely considered in the context of a wider HR and reward strategy, and decisions on pension tend to be made in isolation.

Benefits

A whole plethora of other benefits is often provided by employers. These include medical benefits, cars, discounted shopping and insured and financial benefits. They also include benefits provided at a price that employees would not get if they were not employed by the organisation, such as staff discounts for the employer's products or services. As with pensions, employers rarely take a strategic approach to benefits. Much of it is directed at copying other employers and trying to make sure that what is offered is competitive. The result is that employees are often confused and bamboozled by the range of benefits provided.

When deciding on the benefits to be offered employers should consider three questions:

1. Are there reasons why we want employees to have this benefit? For example, if we wish to take a paternalistic approach to employee wellbeing, is it something we should provide?

2. Can we enable employees to purchase products at a better price or of better quality than they would be able to do for themselves?

3. Does the benefit offered fit with the brand that we want to project as an employer?

For example, many employers offer health and wellbeing benefits to promote a healthy workforce and staff discounts, which enable employees to purchase products and services more cost effectively. These can be good reasons for providing benefits, but when benefits are provided for no better reason than that other organisations provide them, this can lead to additional costs (often relating to administration) and confusion for employees.

Employers often use flexible benefits, enabling employees to choose from a menu of benefits. These arrangements work if the benefits are made available as determined by the questions above. However, such systems can be quite complex to administer, and with the internet age it is not difficult for employees to "shop around" for the benefits that are best suited to them. If the employees trust what the employer is offering, they may feel that they do not need to shop around, but this is a risky approach for employers unless they can be confident in the products offered.

Share incentives

Where companies have quoted shares, they usually encourage employees to own shares in the company. This gives employees a stake in the company and links the value of reward directly with the value of the business. Governments provide tax incentives to increase the level of employee share ownership, and shares can be a cost efficient way to reward employees.

Where the value of the shares is realised over a period of more than one year these are known as Long-Term Incentive Plans (or LTIPs). These are usually provided to executives and are intended to link reward to the creation of long-term shareholder value. So if shareholders get rich, so do the executives.

LTIPs may be in the form of share option plans where there is an option to buy shares in the company on some future date at a fixed price. If the value of the shares has gone up the employee makes a profit when the shares are bought at the lower option price. Usually methods that are more complex are used to define shareholder value and performance, and this is considered further when we discuss Executive Remuneration in Chapter 3.

Quantifying reward

Employers like to let employees know what the reward package is worth, often providing "total reward statements". These summarise the overall value of reward, adding the pay together with the value of bonus potential, share incentives, benefits and pension. The use of such statements has now become standard practice and employees of large companies expect to have them.

The difficulty with total reward statements is that they only include the elements of reward that can easily be valued, so they can only be a partial representation of reward. It is difficult to put a value on training, development and holidays, and some other benefits, and intrinsic reward cannot be quantified.

For the employee total reward statements have little meaning unless there is a point of comparison. To make use of the statement employees need to make comparisons between the total reward they see in the statement and what they might receive from another employer. However, it is not usually possible for them to do this.

Employers also make comparisons between the reward they offer and that of other organisations. These comparisons are part of the process of ensuring that the level of pay is competitive. They can also be used to dispel myths – for example, it is commonly believed that levels of pay in the public sector are not as high as the private sector. This is certainly true for senior roles, but for most public sector roles the reward package is competitive because the pension in the public sector is still far better than in the private sector.

A typical comparison of reward packages is shown below:

Figure 3.   Reward comparisons

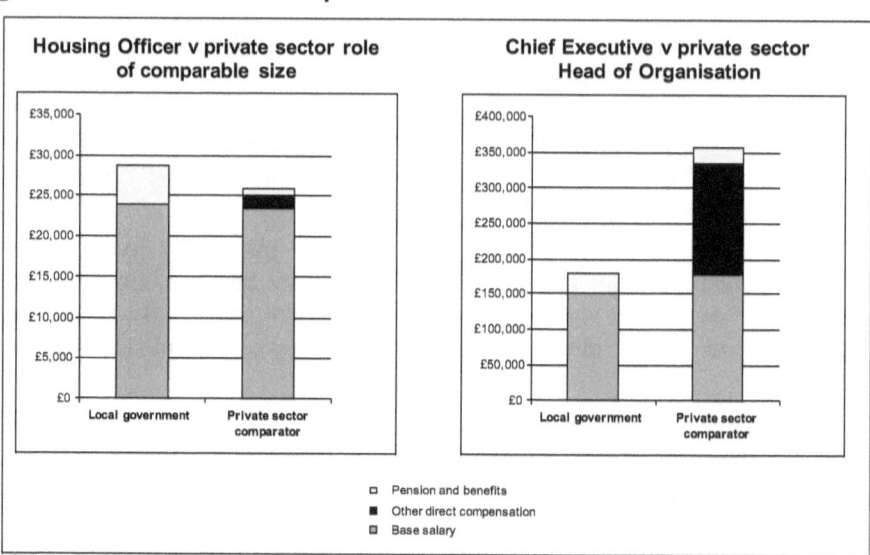

Another problem with valuation is that pay and benefits and extrinsic rewards are only a part of overall reward. It is therefore useful to distinguish between extrinsic and intrinsic rewards:

- **Extrinsic reward** – this is the basic and most visible aspect of reward. It includes money, pension, benefits and share incentives. It also includes training and development, skills development and all the things that an employer will typically provide to attract and retain employees. When designing extrinsic rewards employers seek to match (and where they can, to exceed) the levels of reward offered by other employers.

- **Intrinsic reward** - these are the types of reward that meet psychological needs as described in Chapter 2. It is often the intrinsic rewards, that simply cannot be valued, which really determine whether employees will stay loyal to an employer.

The relationship between the two types of reward is critical to reward management. The best approach is to ensure that the value of extrinsic reward is fair, but to rely on intrinsic reward to differentiate and to retain the people needed.

Chapter 2. Developments in social science

The business world, with its belief that nothing is valid unless it can be measured on a spreadsheet, has been very slow to take up developments in social sciences, and especially in psychology and behavioural economics. Recently in the UK, the Chartered Institute of Personnel and Development (CIPD) produced a detailed Research Report on the behavioural science of reward[4], which described much of the research in this area. This chapter sets out some of the most important development in the social sciences and their implications for reward in the digital age.

The theoretical framework

Reward is still approached through the theoretical framework of neo-classical economics. This is a mythical world in which there is a "buyer" and "seller" (the employer and employee), each with perfect information, perfect trust of one another, and acting out of self-interest as free agents to determine a "price" (the amount of reward). It is a simple and logical way of looking at reward but it is also wrong and can lead to many mistakes.

Few people who are involved in the management of reward and HR believe it actually works like this. Unfortunately, the business world is dominated by accountants, who have been trained in economics, and who tend to think that everything can be explained through numbers. They assume that the market for pay works in much the same way as any other market. They have been trained to believe that money should be used as an incentive, and like to design ever more complicated incentive schemes as part of the reward package. People rarely behave in the way that the spreadsheets used by the accounts department say they should, and this is what makes the management of reward so difficult, and so interesting.

Some of the ideas on labour markets that were developed by Karl Marx are rather more useful. He developed a theory of "alienation". For Marx the worker is alienated from the work that is being done because he has no stake in what is being produced, no autonomy over how it is produced, and is exploited and isolated from other people. The solutions Marx developed are now discredited, but his articulation of one of the potential problems in the employment relationship is correct. Too often The Finance Director's view of the world is that employees are "objects", with reward as the price attached to them, who can be controlled with a mixture of performance management and incentives. This leads to a demotivated and unproductive workforce.

However, the nature of work has changed completely since the time when Karl Marx was writing the Communist Manifesto. Many jobs give the opportunity for autonomy and creativity so that what is produced is "owned" by the employee. In the digital age employers need to make sure that they use these psychologic rewards, and that any threats to them are removed.

Rewards and threats

Neuroscience shows how the brain responds subconsciously to threats and rewards. The reaction to a threat is very different to the response to a reward. Where there is a perceived threat, it is processed as quickly as possible to the exclusion of all other neurological processes. In contrast, rewards are addictive and we are constantly trying find and add to them. This all makes perfect sense in the context of our evolutionary history, and the different reactions to rewards and threats are critical to the way employees respond to reward in the employment relationship.

Pay and the other material rewards are extrinsic reward. Intrinsic reward is when psychological needs are met because they come from within the employee. Intrinsic rewards are potentially more powerful than extrinsic rewards, and are becoming more important in the digital age. This is discussed further in Chapter 4.

The psychological rewards and the potential threats to these are summarised below. The rewards are based on David Rock's SCARF model of basic human needs[5], and the threats are the reverse of these.

Rewards	Threats
Status – Relative position when compared to others	**Disrespect** - anything which suggests reduced social or professional status
Certainty - Knowing what is going to happen in the future	**Uncertainty** – not knowing what is going to happen, especially when something has a personal impact
Autonomy - Choice and freedom to act	**Control** – including having no choices as to what to do, or how to do it and being "micromanaged"
Relatedness - Connections with others and being part of a team	**Isolation** - being alone, with little or no interaction with other people
Fairness - Perception that you and others are being treated fairly	**Injustice** - unfairness, or the perception of unfairness, including situations where the unfairness does not directly impact on oneself

These psychological needs explain much about the way society operates. They create the social norms, which are so important to us and they explain much of our behaviour: Why is it so important to people that they have their own offices? Why is it so much more stressful to wait for a late train if a notice board just says "delayed" without specifying the time when it is due? Why don't shops vary prices depending on how busy the shop is, or what they think a customer can afford to pay? Why does it matter so much to an employee who finds out that another employee is underpaid, even though it has nothing to do with her?

The way we react to rewards is very different from the reaction to threats. We need rewards frequently in small incremental amounts. For much of the time employees are not conscious of reward, except when it comes under threat. Pay is most effective when it supports and enables employees to maximise their intrinsic reward, and it causes the most damage when it is a threat to intrinsic reward. Money is a measure of status. Most employees keep score of what they earn and need to be satisfied that it is fair when compared with what others are paid. Pay can also be a threat to intrinsic rewards if the amount paid is less than anticipated, if it is perceived to be inequitable, or if it is a source of uncertainty.

Systematic biases

Although we are not aware of it, most of the decisions we make are unconscious thoughts and intuitions[6]. Most of thinking is based on **heuristics** or mental short cuts, which is known as fast thinking. The thinking we are aware of, or slow thinking, is effortful and has limited capacity. Fast thinking is what enables us to operate for most of the time, but it is also the source of some systematic biases, or errors. These biases are prevalent in many aspects of reward management, and are the reason why so many people have difficulty in thinking logically about reward.

Some of the most important biases and their implications for reward management are described below:

- **Anchoring:** if we already have a number in mind this will unduly influence the thinking on reward. This is why employees can be so easily convinced that they are underpaid if they hear what seems to them to be a comparable job that is paid more. It also explains why it is so damaging to motivation to create expectations of pay increases that are not fulfilled. In any negotiation on pay, an initial proposal (however spurious or unrealistic) is likely to influence the eventual outcome. This is why any good trade unionist will always anchor the negotiations with an initial claim, even though they know that the amount demanded will never be achieved.

- **Availability heuristic:** There is a bias towards information and knowledge that is readily available to us. It is striking in reward management how people are so easily influenced by their experiences of reward (be these positive or negative) in other organisations and allow these to influence their current decisions, even though the circumstances may be very different. It also leads to the belief that pay is "behind the market" if another organisation advertises some jobs at higher salaries. This is why most people believe levels of pay in the private sector are better than in the public sector. Senior pay is certainly far higher in the private sector and because senior pay tends to dominate media coverage of reward, many people will assume that all reward is higher in the private sector.

Another aspect of the availability heuristic is that we ignore "silent evidence". If a few employees are making a noise because they think they are underpaid, it is very easy to fall into the trap of thinking that the whole workforce is underpaid. If 99% of employees are quietly getting on with the job and are quite content with their pay they will be "silent", and this vital fact can easily be overlooked.

- **Confirmation bias**: once we come to believe something, we will be biased in favour of evidence which confirms that belief. This is why it is so important to make a good first impression. If employees come to believe that the pay system is unfair, they will find evidence to support this belief and ignore any evidence to the contrary.

- **Endowment bias:** there is a bias in favour of keeping what you already have, even if it may not be in your interest to do so. This is why change is always difficult and it is a challenge to persuade employees to give up something they are familiar with, even if you are replacing it with something better.

- **Framing** – the context in which information is presented makes a big difference to the way it is perceived. Marketers know how consumer choice is influenced by the range of prices available for similar products. Some consumers will choose the most expensive item, some will go for the cheapest, but most usually go for something in the middle. The point is that people are more influenced by the context in which information is presented to them than the actual price. The same point works for reward. Employees will make judgements about whether reward is fair based on how it compares that of their colleagues and what they might earn in other organisations. This is more important than the absolute amount that is paid.

Because we mostly rely on fast thinking, the brain can only absorb and compute a limited amount of information when dealing with a problem. It never works to give too many choices in reward management. If possible, make it a binary yes/no-type choice. Alternatively, if you know what the right approach should be, present three choices with the one that should be taken in the middle. This is a legitimate way to ensure that good decisions are made.

- **Loss aversion:** our brains are wired to be loss averse, so the impact of losses is far greater than that of gains. The negative impact of a reduction in pay is always greater than the positive impact of an increase. Loss aversion is also important in managing expectations on the level of pay: if I am expecting a 3% increase and actually receive 2%, I will perceive this as a loss. It is the sort of result that could well cause me to leave an organisation because I will feel threatened and undervalued. In contrast, if I am expecting 2% and receive 3%, the impact of the 1% "gain" will not be as great. Initially I would be pleased at the size of the increase, but fairly soon I would forget about it. This is why managing expectations as to the amount of reward is so important.

It is also important to understand why the implementation of change in pay is so difficult. In a case where 90% of employees gain and 10% lose out, it can often happen that the 10% will have a far greater influence than the majority of the workforce. This is because the impact of the loss on the "losers" is greater than the gains for the "winners", even though the amount of the losses may be insignificant when compared with the gains.

- **Myopia Bias:** the difficulty in identifying and valuing future rewards. Related to loss aversion is the fact that we are biased in favour of immediate rewards, rather than deferred rewards, even though the value of the deferred amount may be far greater. This is one of the reasons why Long-term Incentive Plans (LTIPs) do not tend to provide value for money.

- **Narrative bias**: we believe in the coherence of a story as being more important than isolated facts. Usually facts that fit with the story, or narrative, are accepted and anything that does not fit is disregarded. Anyone preparing a report knows this – you develop the story and then muster the facts to support it. Information that does not fit with the story is buried away in the small print, or sometimes left out altogether. If the report does not have a coherent story, it is unlikely to be read, let alone acted on. Management consultants are storytellers in much the same way as writers of fiction. If they are good at their job, they will be using the narrative bias to get things done. This is critical in the management of reward where there is lots of data available. Use the data to tell a story – otherwise nobody will know what to do with it.

- **Pattern seeking**: this is connected to narrative bias - we like to see structures and patterns because the world is generally much more chaotic than we like to believe. If everything is summarised on a lengthy PowerPoint presentation with lots of data analysis, we think we understand it and that we can get others to understand it. We might well succeed in this, but it is often the case that a strong and logical presentation completely misses the point as to what is really going on.

  Pattern seeking is both a strength and a weakness. Parts of this book present patterns and structures on reward and this is done quite deliberately. Without structure and some narrative, it would be impossible to understand the world around us, and without a narrative this book would probably be unreadable. The danger occurs when we fall into the trap of thinking the real world is as neat and tidy as the patterns we use to describe it.

- **Focusing bias:** When we are thinking about something, it becomes disproportionately important simply by virtue of the fact that we are thinking about it[7]. For most employees the level of pay is not something that occupies much of their attention, and the secret of good reward management is to ensure that pay does not become an issue in the business. This is why it is important to have a clear reward strategy that is effectively communicated to employees. The focusing bias also explains why there is so much emphasis on the annual pay review within organisations. Usually these reviews focus on the size of the % increase, with very little attention paid to the actual amounts of salaries and any anomalies that already exist in the organisation.

- **Substitution heuristic:** many mistakes are made when people unconsciously substitute a difficult question with an easier one. This explains the simplistic approach which many employers take to reward management. It is easier to design a process or find some market data to tell you what to do and assume that is the answer to the question as to what to pay people.

Most economists understand that people do not behave in accordance with their models in the real world, but work on the basis that the biases are random so the effects of these do not invalidate the models they use. The realisation that biases are systematic has led to the development of behavioural economics. This provides a theoretical basis to show how these systematic biases affect economic activity, business decision making and reward management.

The systematic biases also enable reward professionals to understand why people find it so difficult to think rationally about reward. We are loss averse, jump to conclusions based on very limited information and create patterns and explanations for everything in the world around us. All of these characteristics enabled us to survive as a species, but they also mean that our brains are unsuited to dealing with something as difficult and sensitive as reward. In the digital age, it is no longer possible to ignore the behavioural aspects of reward management.

Chapter 3. Things that don't work

In Chapter 1 we looked at the basics of how reward is managed. As jobs have become more varied and complicated in the digital age reward management has struggled to keep up. The problems that employers face are that:

- Employees are not engaged through reward,

- Reward is not integrated with talent management and other HR programmes,

- Job evaluation systems, when they are used, have become increasingly complicated and unmanageable,

- Employers rely heavily on market pay data, and this is often an unreliable means of determining pay.

Reward management tools and methodologies have not been able to keep up with the way in which most jobs are carried out: in the 20th century, most of the jobs that people did were clearly defined, with prescribed tasks that could readily be placed into a Roman army-type structure. In places where this did not work the idea of the market rate evolved. This is based on the assumption that every job has a "price" in the external market, and that reward can be managed by identifying the price.

In this chapter, we look in more detail at some of the problems with the use of job evaluation systems, the reliance on market pay data, and the difficulties that employers have in linking pay to performance. We then go on to comment on sales commissions and executive remuneration.

Job evaluation

As we saw in Chapter 1, there are three basic criteria for determining pay: job size, market rate and performance. In the UK, there are contrasting approaches to the adoption of these criteria. Where Trade Unions are influential, which is mostly in the public sector, job size dominates and there is an overreliance on job evaluation systems and the processes that support these. Internal equity is paramount and levels of reward are mostly determined by the job evaluation system.

Thunder Cloud – Managing Reward in a Digital Age

Some organisations use simpler "levelling" criteria to place jobs into grades or levels. This approach is used to place jobs into grades with broad pay bands. Normally market data is used for the determination of actual salaries within the bands.

Full job evaluation is a more complex means of assessing the size of a job. It is a way of objectively assessing the size of the job under set criteria, or factors. Most of these systems use very similar factors although some are far more complex than others. Below are the factors used in Agenda for Change, the NHS job evaluation system[8], which is one of the more complex systems:

Figure 4.   Example job evaluation system

7. Job Evaluation weighting scheme - scoring chart

Factor	Level 1	2	3	4	5	6	7	8
1. Communication and relationship skills	5	12	21	32	45	60		
2. Knowledge, training and experience	16	36	60	88	120	156	196	240
3. Analytical skills	6	15	27	42	60			
4. Planning and organisation skills	6	15	27	42	60			
5. Physical skills	6	15	27	42	60			
6. Responsibility – patient/client care	4	9	15	22	30	39	49	60
7. Responsibility – policy and service	5	12	21	32	45	60		
8. Responsibility – finance and physical	5	12	21	32	45	60		
9. Responsibility – staff/HR/leadership/training	5	12	21	32	45	60		
10. Responsibility – information resources	4	9	16	24	34	46	60	
11. Responsibility – research and development	5	12	21	32	45	60		
12. Freedom to act	5	12	21	32	45	60		
13. Physical effort	3	7	12	18	25			
14. Mental effort	3	7	12	18	25			
15. Emotional effort	5	11	18	25				
16. Working conditions	3	7	12	18	25			

The system appears to be objective. There are 16 factors and within these, there are between 4 and 8 defined levels. Every job is assessed under each level and given a score. The scores are then aggregated to arrive at a total job size. The job size is then used to determine the pay band within which the job should be placed. The system is designed to objectively assess every aspect of every job in the NHS (except for Doctors whose Trade Union would not participate), and to provide a fair and transparent way of determining pay.

Page 24

The problem with this approach is that many jobs in the digital age are unsuited to job evaluation. Modern jobs are broadly defined, flexible and the outcomes achieved matter more that the things that are measured by job evaluation, such as the size of the budget or the numbers of staff managed. This can lead to the "gaming" of job evaluation systems so that job descriptions are written to achieve what is perceived to be a fair reward outcome.

Job size is the size of the job in terms of the level of responsibilities and the skills that are required to carry out the role. It is about the job and not the individual who is carrying out the job. The weakness of job evaluation is that it separates the job from the individual. Job evaluation can work for simple jobs, but it does not work for more complex roles where the skills that an individual brings make a big difference to the way the role is carried out.

The results of job evaluation are often works of creativity, based on complex rules of interpretation, which are only understood by experts, whose interest is in making the process complicated and mysterious. Job evaluation results are presented as documents of objective fact obscuring a high degree of judgement, rather like the annual accounts of company. It is best not to question the validity of the results and to assume that the experts, with their mysterious rules and precedents, have got it right.

The main advantages of job evaluation systems are:

- Some systems, such as those developed by the Hay Group, Mercer or Towers Watson link directly with market pay data. Therefore, job evaluation under one of these systems gives access to market pay data.

- They are the basis that Employment Tribunals use to assess equal pay claims. If jobs are evaluated as being of comparable size under a recognised job evaluation system, then it is unlikely that an equal pay claim will be successful if the employees are paid similar amounts.

In the private sector, job evaluation systems are used for these limited purposes, but they are not open and transparent to employees. They tend to be managed and maintained by reward professionals to give a justification for pay decisions and to support underlying grading structures. It is questionable whether job evaluation systems should have a significant role as a means of determining pay in a digital age because:

- Although they appear to be objective, many of the decisions as to the levels into which jobs should be placed are subjective,

- Once the rules of the system are known job evaluation systems are very easily "gamed", so that job descriptions are often written to achieve the desired outcome,

- They can only measure the size of the job and they do not look at the skills that individuals bring to each job,

- They do not reflect external market rates of pay, for example, where there are skills shortages,

- Administratively, they are burdensome and time consuming to maintain and keep up to date.

For these reasons, job evaluation systems rarely achieve the intended outcomes and they have been discredited in many organisations. However, job size should always have a role in determining pay. Although market pay data may sometimes be a good proxy for job size, it is not reliable for many types of job, as we will see below. More importantly, relatedness and fairness are two of the basic psychological needs that need to be met. This must be done by demonstrating the internal equity of pay, which can only be achieved through some sort of job evaluation system.

Market pay data

The market rate is usually the basis for managing reward for private sector employers. Most companies base their pay systems on market data using grades (or levels). To address the ambiguity between internal equity and the external market the concept of pay bands has evolved. This means that each level within the organisation has a pay band (often referred to as broad bands) into which all jobs at a certain grade are placed. Often the bands are varied for different types of jobs, based on market data. The problems with this approach are:

- The systems are not transparent for employees. It is unusual for employees to be told where in a pay band they are placed, or what they need to do to progress through the bands, and

- Market data is often unreliable and subject to different interpretations.

When employees ask about the how their pay is determined, they are usually told, "We pay the market rate". Sometimes they are told that the upper quartile of the market rate is paid, but never the lower quartile. The concept that there is a market rate of pay gives employers an easy way to answer the question, but it is a little disingenuous. It is questionable whether there is such a thing as a market rate for many jobs in the digital age.

HR consultancies sell market data. Different consultancies often give different market rates for the same job, depending on the types of organisations that subscribe to their databases and the methods they use to match data to jobs. Employers accept the data they get from HR consultancies and do not like to question it too much. They need market data because it is a convenient way to explain pay decisions.

Market data is often used as a justification for increasing pay. If pay is found to be "behind the market", it is usually increased to bring it into line. Market data is also used to confirm that pay should be ahead of the market – strongly performing business will think they should pay ahead of the market because they have the best people and higher pay is justified by performance. Very rarely is market pay data used as a justification for reducing pay. If pay is behind the market, it is increased and if it is already ahead, this is justified by performance - it is a one-way street.

But how valid is it to talk of a market rate for pay at all? There is a labour market but there is no such thing as a unit of labour as traditional economic models would suppose. People are not a homogeneous commodity where the price responds mechanistically to changes in supply and demand. There is a market rate for particular skills, and it is possible to identify the amounts that would be normally be paid for a particular job size. However, this does not capture the many different types of jobs and the different levels of skill that individuals bring with them.

The market is heavily influenced by the supply of employees. Where there is a skills shortage the "winners curse"[9] takes over. If a number of employers are in pursuit of a limited number of people, the successful recruiter will pay more than the other bidders pay, and hence more than the market rate. This is why the wages of sportsmen are so high and it also explains high levels of executive reward.

The idea of a market rate is especially problematic because it takes no account of the value of individual skills and experience. The market value of the highly skilled and experienced individual is greater than for a less skilled individual. Employers will always be prepared to pay more for someone with a strong track record of success. Market data treats all individuals doing the same job as having the same price in the market. For the more complex jobs of the digital age, the value of market data is increasingly meaningless.

The labour market is also inflexible. Even in the digital age individuals do not readily switch from one employer to another and pay can usually only increase rather than reduce. The location of a job is very important in determining what the market rate is. Most market data in the UK is presented on a regional basis and this is usually unhelpful in determining what the market rate for a particular job should be. Within regions there are significant variations caused by differences in employment rates, costs of living, transport links and the availability of skills in particular areas. In remote locations, employers find it easy to retain people, but recruitment is often difficult. For many jobs, a meaningful market rate can only be obtained by looking at the location in which a job will be based, and it is often difficult to obtain meaningful market data for locations.

The question of whether there is a national or local pay market is primarily determined by the number of positions that are available and the size of the job:

Figure 5.   Local and national pay markets

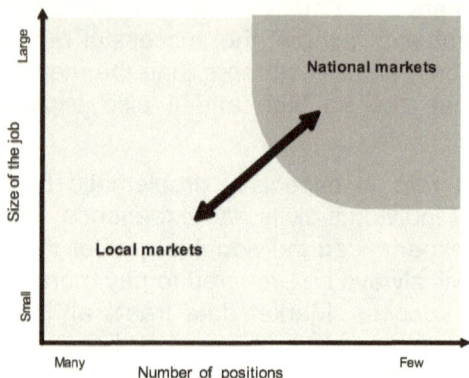

Large jobs where there is a small number of positions tend to have a national rate of pay. This is because employees in these jobs tend to be more mobile. For smaller and less well-paid jobs, markets can be very localised. Factors, such as supply and demand and the strength of local transport links, also have an important role in determining whether the job has a local, regional or national market.

The type of employer also has an impact on rates of pay. Larger employers, and especially organisations which have traditionally been unionised, have higher rates of pay than those of smaller independent businesses.

So why is there this fixation with market rate in the management of reward? It is mainly the substitution heuristic at work – market data simply makes things easier for employers. Pay decisions are always difficult – they involve consideration of internal equity, the external market, and individual performance. They also involve the impact on employee relations and engagement, and deciding what the business can afford. Therefore, employers fall into the trap of substituting the difficult question, "How much should we pay people?" with the much easier one: "What is the market rate?" Providers of market data are on hand to answer the easier question. Employers take the market rate as being the answer to the more difficult question as to what to pay.

However, market data is of some value and there are many jobs where the market rate of pay is relevant and useful. These are jobs where there is a large flexible labour market, where jobs are simple and homogeneous and where individual skill levels are less important.

Almost all markets are imperfect, and there is rarely a single price determined by supply and demand, as is often predicted by neo-classical economics. The labour market is particularly difficult and pay (which is the price in the labour market) is the result of many complex and varying forces.

Where market data is available, it should be considered and used to inform decisions on reward. The danger is in treating market data as if it were the answer as to what to pay employees. This is increasing the case in the digital age for two reasons:

- Jobs are becoming more varied, and what is achieved depends to a large extent on the skills of individual employees, and

- Market data does not take any account of the value of the psychological aspects of the employment relationship. In the digital age, the psychological connection with the employer and the work the employee is doing are the most important aspects of reward.

Pay for performance

Nothing causes more debate and controversy in reward management than the question about whether performance-related pay "works". Economists and accountants are trained to believe in incentives,[10] and they usually believe that if you pay more for something you will get more, and that you will get less if you pay less. This is a simplistic view of the world and does not recognise the complexities of human behaviour. When money is used as an incentive, it is very difficult to predict what the impact will be. Behavioural economics shows how people do not respond to incentives in the way that economic models anticipate. The practical evidence that performance-related pay works in organisations is patchy, to say the least.

Bonus schemes are often designed in the finance department, with complicated calculations and with little regard to whether the scheme will be understood or trusted by employees. It is usually unclear what the bonus is intended to achieve. Sometimes it is implemented for no better reason than that competitors pay bonuses, and the mistaken belief that the bonuses will be an incentive is used to justify its existence.

Very rarely is there a sensible discussion about what performance-related pay is meant to achieve. The Finance Director, who believes in financial incentives, will think it works if the costs of pay vary with business performance. This may be a fair point, but it is equally important to understand the impact on the employment relationship.

Money is addictive. However much the employer pays employees will often come to expect more, and the consequences of not maintaining or increasing the amount of bonus can be severe. More pay for better performance might lead to a short-term boost in performance, but once paid a precedent is set, and the additional money comes to be expected along with yet more money for any further improvements. Few businesses can plan on the basis that they will continually increase the amount paid, even if performance continues to improve. Loss aversion means that the negative impact of paying less than the expectations that have been built up is considerable, even though the actual amount paid may increase.

The debate on performance-related pay also tends to be polarised. People either like it or hate it, and often the views are heavily influenced by personal experiences. Managers tend to favour bonuses because it gives them control of the numbers, and (they hope) a lever to control the employees. Senior managers use spreadsheets and come up with forecasts and ever more complicated performance measures. Even if the schemes work in paying the "right" amount, they rarely work as incentives because employees do not understand them.

The question as to whether pay should be linked to performance therefore depends on two questions:

- Can performance-related pay be used to engage employees and give them a stake in the success of the business?
- Is the job such that it would be unfair if the pay did not take account of individual performance?

The use of individual performance-related pay is examined further in Chapter 6.

Sales commission

For sales jobs, a substantial proportion of reward is usually paid through commissions, often referred to as sales incentives. The employee receives an amount of money based on the number or price of the units sold. The more they sell, the higher the reward. The employer's cost is linked to the level of sales, and the employee is incentivised. It seems like a perfect way to reward employees.

Unfortunately, the system only works well for simple and straightforward sales, where sales activity can easily be quantified, ideally on a daily basis. The employee needs to understand exactly what she will be paid if she sells 100 units in a week and how much more she will get if she sells 120 units. Here, there is a clear incentive to maximise sales, and the employer knows what the cost of the commission will be for a given level of sales.

In the digital age, very few sales are as simple as this. The way sales are managed has changed, and commission-based models of reward are struggling to keep up. The changes include:

- The traditional asymmetry of information between the buyer and the seller is breaking down. Usually information is readily available to buyers and they are well informed as to what they need. The advantage that the salesman used to have in terms of knowledge of the product is much diminished.

- Marketing and business development functions have a more powerful role in organisations. Often the successful sales functions depend on the marketing strategy, rather than the effectiveness of the salesforce.

- Customer relationships have become increasingly important. The strength of long-term relationships with customers cannot be measured through traditional commission-based schemes.

- In complex sales, such as in financial services, the financial incentive to achieve a sale can easily lead to the customer being misled. The history of miss-selling financial services products has exposed the discrepancy between the complexity of the products and the simplistic sales commission structures that were usually in place.

Employers have tried to respond to these difficulties by developing increasingly complex, but mechanistic, approaches to sales commissions. Many schemes have become so complicated as to be almost unmanageable, creating uncertainty (a psychological threat) and losing the line of sight between the activity and the reward. Sales commission plans rarely work as "incentives", in the correct meaning of that word. For many types of sales employers would do better to replace commissions with higher levels of salary and annual bonus.

Executive Remuneration

Executive remuneration attracts more media coverage than any other area of reward, and psychology, which is one of the themes of this book, explains the high levels of remuneration for executives. An executive who believes that her level of remuneration is similar to what she could earn for the same effort elsewhere is likely to think that her pay is fair. The ability to make fair comparisons is more important than the absolute amount of pay, and the psychological need for status dominates.

If the needs for status and fairness are satisfied, levels of pay will not influence the behaviour of executives. It is only when remuneration is not perceived to be fair in comparison to others that the amount becomes an issue. If it were possible to systematically reduce executive remuneration across the board by (say) 25%, this would not have any real impact on the performance of companies or the calibre of executive talent that is available. Executives would still do the same jobs in the same way as they did when they were on higher levels of remuneration.

The problem of identifying a market rate of pay is particularly acute for executives. There is a limited supply of executives at the top level because of the very cautious approach to making appointments. There is also little incentive for the buyer (in this case the Board of the company) to offer the most appropriate price. The risk of not making the right appointment, in terms of the impact on share price, is usually far greater than the risk of paying too much. Often paying too much enables the Board to put a positive spin on the appointment: "We needed to pay a lot to get the best possible candidate" they will say.

Candidates will not move to a new role unless a premium is paid over the "market rate" to compensate for the risk of moving. If there is a market at all in executive remuneration, it is like an auction in the arts market with very high prices being paid for highly desirable and over-hyped works of art. Moreover, it has the added complexity that the work of art has an interest in, and a big influence on, the price that is paid for it!

A great deal of creativity goes into trying to disguise and justify levels of executive remuneration, and the ubiquitous use of LTIPs and share incentives is the most obvious example. The description of an LTIP as an "incentive" implies that the executive will make better decisions and put in more discretionary effort than would otherwise be the case. This is not credible: many executives do not understand the detail of how their LTIP operates. They seek to make the best decisions and maximise their effort, regardless of the financial reward that might be available, provided the overall package is seen as being fair.

If the stated purpose of an LTIP is simply to align the reward of executives with shareholder returns, this may well be sensible. However, this is rarely the sole or the main purpose of using an LTIP: usually they are couched in the language of incentives and individual performance. LTIPs cannot operate as incentives for improved individual performance because they are too complicated and the performance measures are too remote. Most executives have little interest in the detail of how their LTIP operates and they cannot usually see how they are doing against target performance at any point in time. The prospect of an uncertain reward in the future means that LTIPs are undervalued by executives, or that the employer has to commit to pay more than is necessary. This is due to the myopia bias explained in Chapter 2.

The requirement that companies should be more transparent about their remuneration is unlikely to help. It is arguable that this actually increases the pressure for higher levels of remuneration because it makes it easier for companies and their executives to compare themselves with their peers.

A more activist shareholder approach is also unlikely to work. Investors and their representatives will always be less well informed, and therefore, a step behind the company – it is always possible to find good reasons for increasing remuneration, but it is very difficult to reduce it.

High levels of executive remuneration are not simply the result of greed or incompetence. Nobody can be blamed and there is little that can be done about it. It is the result of normal human behaviour. Everything is easily explained by the fact that executives, Remuneration Committees, their advisors, shareholders, politicians and those trying to regulate executive remuneration are humans. They have the same psychological needs that we all do, and they are subject to the same biases and mistakes.

Nevertheless, more should be done to challenge the many disingenuous ways that executive remuneration is presented. There is no "market rate" for executive roles any more than there is a market rate for a Picasso that has just fetched a high price in an auction. LIPTs are not incentives – if they work at all, it is in linking remuneration to shareholder value.

Most importantly of all, no executive is worth 180 times more than the average worker[11] in terms of the personal contribution that they can make. Executives share the same genome as the rest of humanity, and like everyone else, they only have 24 hours in a day and need to sleep sometimes. Remuneration is not at astronomical levels because the individual executive is worth the money. If a respected Chief Executive with a strong track record is not in place to lead the company, the share price falls. A strong track record means that the executive is likely to have been consistently lucky. There is a limited supply of executives because it is often only the lucky ones who make it to the shortlist, and individuals of high calibre who have been less fortunate are excluded.

The subject of this book is reward for the wider workforce, where most of the work is done, and this section is all it has to say about executive remuneration. Executive remuneration will continue to be the cause of much envy, negative press coverage, and be the source of much public anger and political activism. However, the problem will always be with us if we are to have publically listed companies and require human primates to lead them.

Part 2 - Reward for a digital age

Chapter 4. Re-defining reward

How work is changing

Information is now available in a way that would have been unimaginable at the end of the last century. It is not just the volume of information that is important – we have also developed revolutionary ways of managing and sharing information. This has resulted in dramatic changes to the types of jobs that people are doing and a need to rethink the nature of the employment contract.

Employees now have access to commentary on information through the internet and social media and they can participate in that commentary. Social media has created a new culture of openness and information sharing, and employers need to understand how this changes the employment relationship. In the past pay was not talked about, hidden away like a dirty secret, but attitudes like this are changing.

Regulatory changes have also led to a greater culture of openness. For example, in the UK it is no longer lawful for employers to require employees to keep their salaries confidential. Employers are now required to disclose their gender pay gap, and listed companies will soon need to disclose the ratio between their top and average salaries.

The latest generation of HR systems, using "cloud" technology, enables employers to interact with employees in new ways. Intranet content can be tailored to the needs of individual employees, and digital lines of communication make it much easier for managers and employees to communicate with each other. These developments should lead organisations to become more open and transparent about reward – employees now expect better information, and technology enables this to be provided.

Sometimes these changes are characterised as generational differences. There is much talk about the different needs of the latest generation, labelled Generation Y, and the different approaches that are needed to engage with this new generation of employees. It is certainly true that Generation Y are better attuned to the digital age and social media, and are more likely to be intrinsically motivated in their work.

These changes affect the whole of society. What we are seeing is the latest generation being quicker to engage with the changes because it is less attached to the traditional way of doing things. The idea that each generation has different needs because they are a new generation is probably an illusion. This comes from the fact that the older generation has "grown up", and forgets that it was pretty much the same at the same age. Most social change comes from technological and economic developments, and not because each generation somehow sees the world differently.

For employers the employment contract is valuable because it places obligations on the employee, and if it is managed correctly, it will secure a level of commitment and loyalty, which would not exist outside the employment relationship. For employees the relationship meets the psychological needs of certainty (with regular pay) and relatedness.

The psychological aspects of the contract are now more important than they ever were. Much of the work that is carried out in an employment framework could be undertaken without an employment contract, as can be seen in the growth in the use of agency staff and contingent labour[12]. As the psychological aspects of the relationship become more important, employers should be placing these at the heart of the way they engage with employees, and reward should be a part of this. If they fail to do this, they will not get loyalty and commitment and there would be no value in employing people.

Before the digital age, most work was drudgery, and people went to work solely because they were paid and needed the money. Marx, writing in the middle of the 19th Century, was quite right to identify the alienation that many people felt about their work, and this is one of the reasons why Marxism became such a popular political philosophy. Jobs are now much better attuned to the psychological needs of employees, and it is probably the social change that has come from this that did more than anything else to put an end to communism.

Reward management has yet to catch up with the digital age and much of it is little changed from the Roman army approach. It assumes clearly defined jobs within a hierarchical structure, and employees are paid for the activities that they carry out. In the 20th century most jobs were comprised of prescribed tasks. These were set out in the job description (often at great length) and the work was managed according to those tasks. It was clear what the tasks of the job should be, and it was clear what should be paid for the work.

In the digital age, most jobs depend on the capabilities of the employee. They require innovation, the building of relationships, and the outcomes from the job cannot be achieved by following a set of pre-defined rules. Employees decide how to use the knowledge and skills they have to achieve the required outcomes. This has some important implications:

- The traditional methods of managing reward, through job evaluation and the use of market pay data no longer work.

- The potential for intrinsic reward is unlocked. The value of extrinsic reward, such as pay, becomes just a part of overall reward.

- There is a need for more openness and transparency. Organisations that are able to achieve this, and design reward so that it supports the psychological needs of employees, will gain a competitive advantage.

Does pay still matter?

The purpose of pay has changed. Once pay exceeds a minimum level it rarely makes a significant practical difference to people's lives in the digital age. A century ago, additional pay might mean a better diet, not having to make old clothes last for quite so long, or perhaps even going out to the cinema. Changes in what people were paid made a real practical difference.

In the digital age, higher pay usually means that what is already a good lifestyle (by historic standards) becomes even better. Additional money is used to spend on luxuries rather than essentials. If there is always enough food in the house and some spare money to spend, people are more likely to visit an expensive restaurant. However, if you are hungry, an expensive meal in a restaurant does not seem much better than something basic cooked at home. If people can afford to they will often pay a lot more than they need to for a branded luxury good, even when a less expensive choice performs exactly the same function.

In the digital age, pay has a dual purpose. It should firstly take care of the practical material needs of employees, and the second purpose is meet the psychological need for the status and luxuries that higher pay brings. Even in the earlier part of a career, when employees tend to set themselves milestones, such as owning the first car, or the first house, the impact of these is largely psychological. There is a minimum level of pay that is needed for essentials and the purpose of most of pay in the digital age is to:

- Give access to luxuries and lifestyle choices, and
- Differentiate reward within an organisation so that roles that are more senior are paid more.

This does not mean that pay is not important. The psychological purpose of pay is as important, and is certainly more complicated, than the first practical material purpose. The amount of extrinsic reward in itself may not be important, but it can easily become a threat to the more powerful intrinsic rewards. Reward professionals spend most of their time worrying about whether pay is in line with "the market" but they should be asking if it:

- Meets the expectations of individual employees?
- Recognises career progression and the acquisition of new skills?
- Is seen as fair by employees?
- Supports collaborative working with colleagues?

If the answer to any of these questions is "no" there is a potential threat to employees' psychological needs, and pay has the potential to do great damage. If the answers to the questions are all "Yes", and if pay is affordable for the employer, the reward strategy would be perfect, although this probably never happens in the real world. The secret of good reward management is in being aware of the areas where it can be a threat and cause damage, and to minimise these in a way that is affordable for the employer.

Reward is part of an employment contract and is what employees get in return for their time and effort. It is also part of a wider employment relationship, which works best as a psychological contract. Employers are slow to recognise this - the business world is dominated by accountants, lawyers, and by the management of systems and processes. Psychology is still seen as too fluffy and a little dubious, but progress in social science in recent decades has started to change this.

Using intrinsic reward

Reward includes both extrinsic and intrinsic rewards. Intrinsic reward, which meets the psychological needs described in Chapter 2, is as important as extrinsic reward. Good reward management involves managing both types of reward and ensuring that they are aligned with each other, and support the wider employment relationship.

So how can the employer provide intrinsic and psychological rewards? The first way to do this is by recognising that humans are social creatures. Being with people who we like and get on with is the greatest source of happiness for many of us, and although most social contact takes place outside the work environment, it is an increasingly important part of modern work. Often it is what makes people want to come into work and prevents them from leaving a particular employer. Good employers will make space for social contact between employees (within and outside the work environment) because it helps to build a strong team culture, and makes people work more effectively together. It meets the basic psychological need for relatedness.

The intellectual challenge that comes from solving problems and working towards goals is often an important driver in keeping people at work, and in making them work more effectively. Our brains are wired to try to solve problems. Even if we are unsuccessful, we often find pleasure in the task of problem solving. We also like to have a purpose and to set ourselves personal goals to be achieved. In many jobs, work provides a sense of purpose for people's lives. The ability to solve problems and the sense of purpose meets the psychological need for status and autonomy.

Work also brings the altruistic pleasure that comes from helping other people with their problems. This is an important feature of jobs in health and social care, and also in many customer and professional services roles. We have an innate need for the society in which we live to be fair, both to ourselves and to others. Many jobs enable the psychological need for fairness and for helping other people to be fulfilled.

Employment, with the legal framework that surrounds it, offers a measure of stability and certainty to employees. The employment contract with regular work and regular pay meets the psychological need for certainty.

In the digital age, it is now possible for employers to mobilise all aspects of intrinsic reward and meet the basic psychological needs of employees through their work. If you ask someone "How are you getting on at work?", and they are able to confirm that they are getting on well and perhaps enjoying it, they usually highlight intrinsic rewards as being the main contributors to this. They will talk about how they are getting on with colleagues and customers, whereas it is unlikely that they will refer to pay or other extrinsic rewards.

The respective roles of extrinsic and intrinsic rewards are different. Extrinsic rewards are a baseline and without them organisations would not be able to employ people. The baseline needs to be fair, both in terms of comparisons within the organisation and with other employers. If the level of extrinsic reward is not seen to be fair, it grows in importance and the impact of intrinsic reward will be lost. This is known as **crowding out**[13]. Extrinsic rewards are more visible and their value can be more easily quantified. This visibility means that they tend to dominate our thinking on reward. The availability heuristic and the focussing illusion take over.

One of the problems with the businesses world is that it tends to concentrate on the things that can be easily measured. The availability heuristic means that we look for solutions in the information that is readily available to us. We simply do not look for information that is not readily available, and which cannot be easily understood. The intrinsic rewards cannot be measured; they are mysterious and affect individual employees in different ways. For these reasons, they are too often ignored.

It has become common in HR to talk of the Employment Value Proposition (EVP) in an attempt to bring together all of the things that the employer offers to the employee. Most models of EVP are a checklist of the things that can be used to reward employees. The model of reward that is used in this book to distinguish between intrinsic and extrinsic reward is shown below:

Figure 6.   **A model of reward**

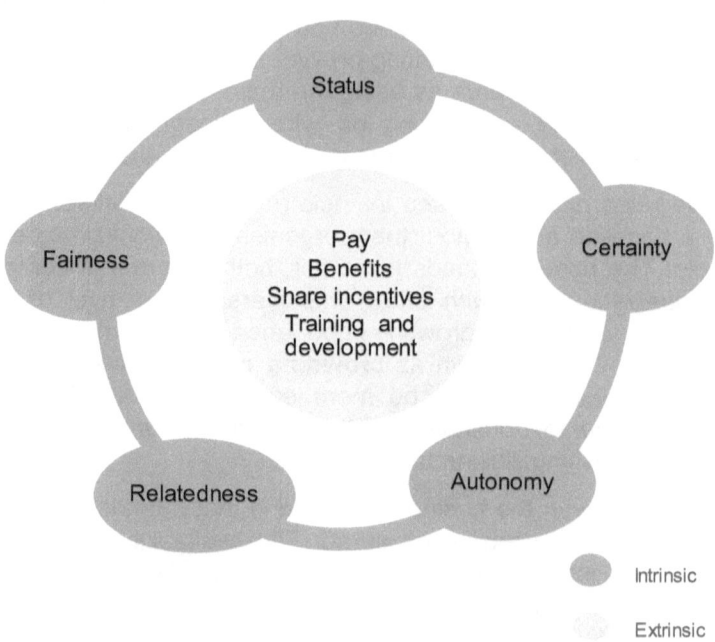

Great expectations

In a world where intrinsic rewards have become more important, do the extrinsic rewards still matter? Could it be that the best approach is to have these as a baseline, leave them alone, and to concentrate on maximising the value of intrinsic rewards?

Extrinsic rewards do matter because if they are not managed carefully they will come to dominate the intrinsic rewards. The intrinsic rewards will be crowded out and will cease to be effective. It is a very simple concept to understand: ask someone "How they are getting on at work?" and if they were not paid the amount they were expecting to get in the last month, this fact is likely to dominate their response and the intrinsic rewards will be irrelevant.

As an employee it is important to me that I have status, and that I am rewarded fairly for what I do. I will not think much about reward if it is not a threat to these psychological needs. However, if I perceive that there is an inconsistency this becomes a threat. The intrinsic reward is crowded out, and the fact that I am not paid what I think I am worth becomes important, not so much because of the amount of money, but because of the threat that I am feeling. This is not a rational response, but it is the way people respond if the reward does not meet expectations. The threat is likely to be even more pronounced if there is a reward strategy in place which says the employer is committed pay between the median and upper quartile of the market. If I think my employer has failed to do this they will have broken their promise to me and this will be a threat.

Once my mind is made up about this, it is unlikely that I will ever be persuaded that I am wrong. The confirmation bias takes over, and I will start to look for evidence that I am right: I will find out what others are paid and get some market data to show that I am underpaid. Because of the confirmation bias, I will only see the evidence to support my case and nothing else.

There are only two ways in which my employer can deal with this problem. They can pay me what I think I should be paid (the expensive option!), or they can manage my expectations before I get into this situation.

The communication of reward is as important as getting the amount right. What usually matters most is whether the amount of pay fits with expectations. Reward, like so much of business, is managed by looking at the numbers and takes little account of the psychological impact of what is done. Reward should provide certainty and meet expectations. It should be treated in the same way as any other customer relationship: if a customer expects a response within two days and it takes a week they will not be a happy customer. If the response takes a week when it is expected to take two weeks, there will be a happy customer. The level of service is exactly the same and all that has been done is to change expectations.

It is the same with reward. We do not like uncertainty and the potential for unpleasant surprises because they are a threat. Managing reward should be about building confidence and managing expectations. Most reward professionals put their efforts into getting the amounts right and managing the expectations of Finance Director. Rarely is enough thought given to ensuring that expectations of employees are in line with what the business is able to pay.

The impact of falling short of employee expectations is always greater than the impact of exceeding them because of loss aversion. This is illustrated below:

Figure 7.   Managing expectations

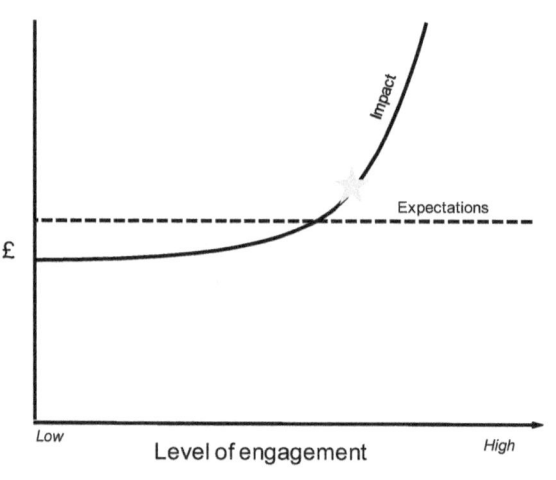

This brings out a fundamental point in reward management. The impact of a bonus of £10,000 is unlikely to be greater than the impact of bonus of £5,000 if the employee is expecting these amounts in both cases. The impact of the money comes from how the amount compares with expectations, and this is especially the case if the amount is less than expected. A good reward strategy could be defined as always ensuring that the amount paid is slightly ahead of expectations. The challenge is in knowing what the expectations are and managing them to ensure that they fit with what the business can afford.

The psychological reward of steady pay increases in line with expectations over two years will be positive. An increase that exceeds expectations in Year 1, followed by an increase that falls short of expectations in Year 2, will have a negative psychological impact. Even though the overall amount paid might be more than would paid through steady increases, the negative impact of in year 2 will crowd out the positive impact of the overall increase.

The value of money is often perceived to be greater if it is paid in incremental amounts. Our brains evolved to hoard and calculate how we are doing. Due to the myopia bias, small and regular bonuses also work better than large irregular bonuses. Ask yourself a simple question: assume zero interest rates and inflation and that you have to choose between taking:

a) £10,000 now, or

b) An unspecified sum a year from now.

How much would b) need to be before you took it?

For most people the answer will be a lot more than £10,000 because of the delay in getting the money.

The recent drive for deferring bonuses in the financial services industry might be useful from a risk management perspective, but the psychology of it is very likely to lead to larger bonuses being paid. This is also why long term incentive plans are not an effective reward vehicle, as discussed in Chapter 3.

In the digital age, employers need to change the way they think about reward. Historically most of the emphasis has been on extrinsic rewards, with intrinsic rewards getting very little attention. Usually the intrinsic rewards are dealt with separately, almost as an afterthought, under the banner of "communications" or "employee relations". This book argues that the intrinsic rewards are as important as the measurable extrinsic rewards. A good reward design should strengthen extrinsic rewards to ensure that crowding out does not happen, and we move on to show how this can be done in the following chapters.

Chapter 5. Pay framework design

The basis for reward design is usually a pay framework based on the grades and levels in the organisation. Pay frameworks, commonly referred to as pay structures, usually fall into one of two types:

- The traditional, rigid and inflexible structure based on job evaluation. This is derived from the Roman army model and is open and transparent.

- Broad banded pay structures based on market rates of pay. This involves setting pay bands for each grade, with pay being set based on performance and market rate within the band.

Broad banded pay structures are not really structures at all. They give the illusion of structure and are of little practical use in controlling costs or enabling employees to understand how pay is determined. Pay frameworks usually include some element of performance-related pay, and this is discussed further in Chapter 6.

Reward is a cloud and pay structures are clocks. They never work as neatly and tidily as they look on paper, and sometimes they are misleading attempts to give the appearance of a structure where none exists. In this book, we use the term pay framework, which gets away from the idea that reward can have a rigid structure. A pay framework consists of the rules and processes through which pay decisions are made. It should show how pay fits with the structure of the organisation and it should also include the underlying language to explain how pay is determined.

It is possible to make individual pay decisions without a formal pay framework. Some small organisations do this successfully, but larger employers need some sort of pay framework to manage reward. A good pay framework enables employers to:

- Make rational pay decisions, that are consistent within the organisation,

- Communicate with employees so they can understand how pay is determined, and

- Ensure that the costs of pay are consistent with business results.

The difficulties in relying on market pay data and job evaluation are described in Chapter 3. These methods are not usually understood by employees and can easily be a threat to the psychological needs of employees. They create uncertainty, and often fail to meet expectations. This is partly because reward is hidden away and shrouded in secrecy in most organisations.

Employers cling to the fallacy that pay decisions are based on objective processes and evidence. The reality is that most of reward has to be managed through the exercise of judgement. The level at which jobs should be evaluated; the interpretation of market pay data and the assessment of individual performance, all involve the exercise of difficult judgements. This is unavoidable, but the reluctance to be open about how the process really works can be the source of a great deal of mistrust between employers and employees.

This chapter sets out an approach to designing pay frameworks in the digital age. It moves away from the idea of using job evaluation or market rate to mechanistically determine pay, and advocates the use of informed judgement in making pay decisions. It also shows how pay frameworks should be designed to fit with the different types of jobs that employees are doing. If pay frameworks are designed in this way and communicated effectively, they will be better trusted by employees.

The rate for the job

It is best to be open about the fact that reward is an art and not a science because pay cannot be determined solely by mechanistic processes. It is preferable to use the term "**rate for the job**" rather than market rate. The rate for the job is informed by market data where it can be relied on, but it should also be based on job size and internal equity. It is the amount that the employer determines should be paid for a particular job, on the basis that the job is being carried out to the required standard. It should also be applied equitably within the company, but it should not seek to replicate rates of pay offered in other organisations.

Most companies link their rates of pay to a particular source of market pay data, and tell their employees that they are paying the "market rate". It is unhelpful to do this in a mechanistic way because different sources of market pay data often give different market rates for same job. A better approach is to look at market data from a variety of different sources and to form a judgement about what the rate for job should be for the organisation.

The illustration shows a range of market pay for each job size:

Figure 8.   Example of segmentation of rates for each job

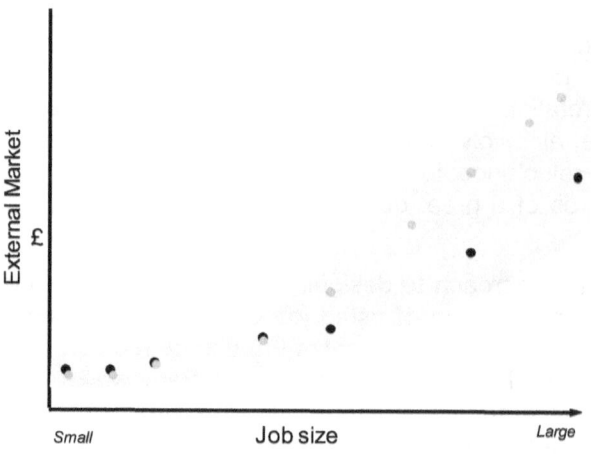

- ● Segment A – Rate for the job
- ○ Segment B – Rate for the job

The illustration shows two job families, or **segments** of jobs, Segment A and Segment B. Actual market rates for jobs in these segments are different, even though they have the same job size. A rate for the job is determined based on both market data and job size. For jobs where the market shows little difference in pay the rates for the job in each segment are identical. As the market rates diverge, (the market rates for jobs in Segment B are higher than Segment A) the rate for the job differs between the segments. This is a far better approach than to devise a single pay band to cover each segment. If this was done, the full market rate of pay might not be paid for Segment B, or alternatively employees in Segment A might have expectations of higher pay, which cannot be realised. The illustration does not show the impact of performance on pay, which is a further criterion that could be used to vary pay.

The rate for the job model has one great advantage over the pay bands that are used by most employers: it makes it possible to explain clearly and openly to employees how their pay is determined and to manage their expectations as to how it will progress in the future. This approach is much better than fitting salaries into a broad pay band, which is determined by market data, and then being unable to explain to employees why they are positioned where they are in the band. These (so-called) pay structures usually lead to psychological threats with perceptions of unfairness and uncertainty, and they make it more difficult for employers to control costs.

Annual pay reviews

The rate for the job should also be adjusted upwards for annual pay increases. The adjustment should be based on trends in annual salary increases and does not need to be tied into particular movements in market data. In times of low inflation, both employers and employees attach far too much importance to annual pay reviews. Reward management degenerates into discussions about whether the percentage pay increase should be 2.5% or 2.75%, often driven by what is going into the business plans for the next year. Little is done before the announcement of the final figure to identify the expectations of employees, and the increase usually does nothing to address any internal inequities that already exist. Usually the annual pay increase only matters as a point of comparison – if the increase is less than that provided by competitors, it will send a negative message.

The availability heuristic gives the percentage increase unwarranted importance and it can have a big psychological impact. It is an easy point of comparison for employees and makes a visible difference to pay from one month to the next. It is also information that is readily available; it is much more difficult for employees to get meaningful information on how their pay compares with the external market or with that of colleagues. The annual increase will always be an important part of reward management, but employers should do more to manage expectations on the level of the annual increases. Expectations are best managed by connecting reward to **talent**

models, the process of which will be discussed in the following parts of this chapter.

Segmenting jobs

Employees need to understand how reward connects with the types of jobs that they are doing, with their career progression and the contribution they are making to the employer. If reward is not connected with these things, it is likely to be perceived as unfair, and could become a threat. If an employee expects to be rewarded for the exceptional contribution they make or the additional skills, experience or qualifications gained, a failure to deliver on this will also be viewed as a threat.

Most employers manage talent through the use of performance management, **career paths**, training and development programmes. Reward needs to fit into this wider picture if it is to make sense to employees. Most pay structures do not do this, and where they do, this tends to happen by accident rather than design. Often employers adopt a "one size fits all" approach and this leads to problems such as:

- Pay progression arrangements and career paths which cannot be fulfilled,

- Pay that does not reward the added value that capable individuals bring to some types job, and

- A lack of pay progression for jobs where it is important to retain employees in the same job for a number of years.

In most large organisations, different approaches to talent management apply to different types of jobs, or **segments** of the workforce. The workforce should be segmented with reference to the different jobs in the organisation and the different **talent models** that apply to them. The reward framework should be designed to fit with the talent model that relates to the job.

Employers are sometimes reluctant to adopt a segmented approach because it is seen as divisive, and also may seem complicated. Therefore, they adopt the approach that works best for the majority of employees, apply this to the whole workforce, and then indulge in some tinkering to adapt pay for particular segments where they think it is necessary. This often ends up being more divisive and complex than it would be if they adopted a segmented approach in the first place.

If reward is unconnected with different ways in which talent is managed, it creates ambiguous messages for employees and can become unaffordable for the employer. If there is no clear framework as to how pay progression should operate costs are very likely to get out of control.

There are four possible talent models, each of which points to a different approach to how pay should be designed:

Figure 9.   The four talent models

Talent Model   **How pay should be structured**

Talent Model	Description	How pay should be structured
Career model	Long-term career opportunities are available for those who develop within the career path	A pay framework that rewards expertise and progression through the career path
Market model	Skills are available in the external labour market and long-term career opportunities with the employer are limited	A single rate of pay aligned with the external market
Retention model	Specialist skills are required for the job and these are not readily available in the external market.	Lower starting pay increasing incrementally as the employee gains in expertise in the same job
Contribution model	The job is flexible/broadly defined and the capabilities of the employee have a large impact on results achieved	Pay is varied by reference to the contribution that the employee makes

The starting point in pay framework design should be to look at different talent characteristics of jobs. This is best examined by considering four questions:

1. **Does the job require skills that can readily be purchased in the external labour market?** This question is about whether the skills needed for the job can readily be bought in from other organisations, or whether they are best developed within the employer.

2. **Is there a career path?** It is necessary to consider whether or not the job fits in a structured career path and whether there is an expectation that the individual will progress to a higher skilled job within the organisation. It is important that there should be realistic expectations of progression, linked to professional qualifications or experience gained in the lower parts of the career structure.

3. **Is the job complex?** There is a need to consider whether the skills needed to be fully effective in the job can be developed within weeks or months, or whether they can only be acquired as a result of many years of training and/or experience. It is important to consider what the difference in pay should be between an inexperienced jobholder who is new to the role, and an experienced jobholder who is performing the role to a high standard. For more complex jobs there should be a large difference in the amounts that are paid, based on what is felt to be fair for the different levels at which the job is carried out.

4. **How self-directed are the activities of the job?** In some jobs, the tasks are tightly defined and the jobholder has limited autonomy on the activities. Other jobs are self-directed and the way the job is carried out depends very much on the approach taken by the jobholder. This is linked to question 3, but it is not the same question – some jobs require considerable technical expertise and are very complex (for example, lawyers, scientists and clinicians), but often they are quite narrowly defined, and the expertise and advice are provided on the issues presented to the jobholder.

These questions should be applied to the job and not to the individual jobholders. If the questions are applied to the characteristics that individual jobholders bring to their roles, the answers become too complex because of the different skills and aspirations of individuals, and it is not practical to design pay structures around the different needs to individuals. Employers should link pay structures to the characteristics of jobs and design pay frameworks that fit with the talent models in the business. Using the questions above the following flow chart can be used as a guide to allocating jobs between the four talent models shown in Figure 9

Figure 10.   Allocating jobs to talent models

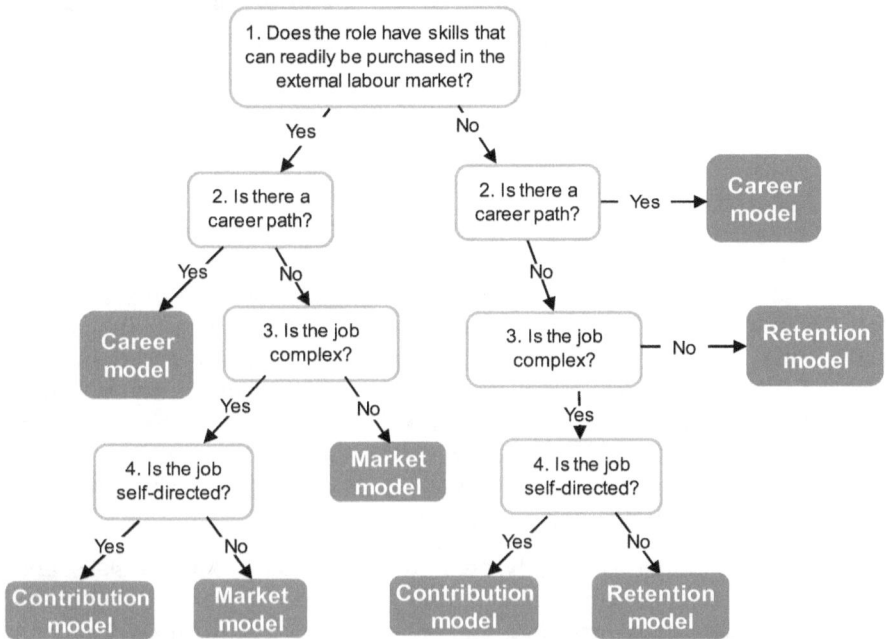

Employers should consider the questions in Figure 10 to understand how the talent models should apply to each segment of the workforce. Although the process appears complicated, it should be fairly straightforward to run through the questions as a list of the points that need to be considered. Most employers will find that two or three different talent models apply to their jobs and should use this as the basis for the design of a pay framework.

Design of pay frameworks

The pay framework should fit with the different talent models and employers with more than one talent model should adopt a segmented approach. There is no precise answer as to how pay frameworks should exactly be designed, and a judgement needs to be made as to what is the best approach for each employer. In many instances, the best approach should be determined by the capacity that the employer has for managing the pay framework, including their capability to assess individual skills and performance. The following paragraphs show some ideas as to how pay frameworks could be designed to fit with each of the four talent models.

The **Career Model** simply requires that the pay structure should reflect the career path. Care must be taken in determining whether there is a career path, and it is easy to fall into the trap of designing career paths for every job in the organisation.

Career paths can be an illusion, and this often leads to mistakes in reward design. We tend to see only the people who have moved towards the top of the ladder (the availability heuristic), and assume that there is a neat and tidy progression from top to bottom. We do not see all the people who fell, or jumped off, the ladder before they go near the top[14]. It is easy to make the mistake of thinking there is a career path, when the reality is very different. Jobs should only be treated as fitting into the career model if employees have a reasonable prospect of progressing from one role to the next. The career model does not apply to jobs towards the top of the career path where realistic prospects of further promotion may not exist.

There should be a series of clearly defined roles setting out the skills and experience that are required for each level. This should include definition of the necessary qualifications, training, and development that is needed for jobs in each level in the career path. Movement from one job to the next within the path should depend on defined promotion criteria, and there should be a business need for the more advanced role to be carried out before a promotion can take place.

Pay progression within each job in the career path should also be based on an assessment of the individual's skills and experience to carry out the job. The following is an example of a pay framework for a career model:

Figure 11.   The career model

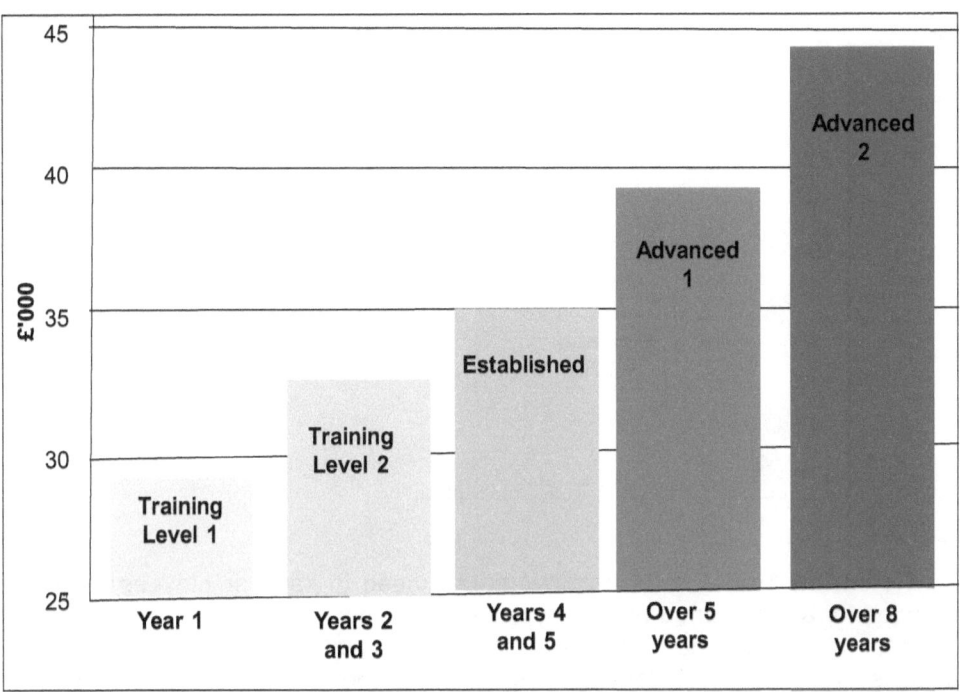

The career model only works where there are enough employees within the career path to give every employee a reasonable opportunity to progress, at least to the Established level. The model works best for professional groups where there are large numbers of incumbents and where qualifications and professional experience readily enable employees to be placed at their correct level in the career path.

The **Market Model** should be based on spot rate for the job, which is determined primarily by the external employment market. For employees who are developing into the job there should usually be a developing range of pay below the rate for job. Each employee should be aware of what they need to do to develop to the full rate for the job, and there should be a plan in place to show how they can achieve this.

Figure 12.   The market model

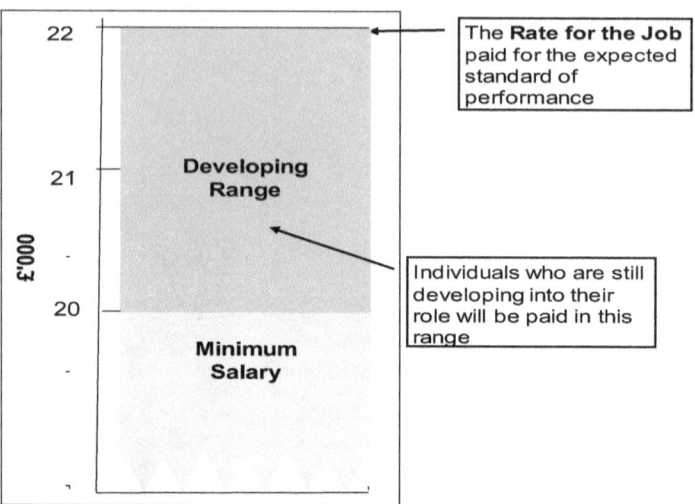

The **Retention Model** is for employers who need to keep employees in the same job for a long period of time, typically more than three years. This model works for jobs where the skills are not readily available in the external market so it is necessary to develop them within the organisation. In these circumstances, steady pay progression can be offered within the same job, subject to the performance of the employee meeting expectations. The traditional Retention Model is achieved through an incremental pay scale and this is a basically sound model if:

- It is affordable, in that not all employees end up towards to the top of the pay range. This requires that there should be a reasonable number of employees in the organisation so the "churn" of employees enables the cost of those at the top of the pay range to be funded by less expensive employees lower down the range.

- Progression through the pay ranges is subject to satisfactory performance being achieved. This means that the majority of employees can expect to progress on an annual basis, but that any who are not performing to the required standard do not progress.

An illustration of the loyalty model is shown in Figure 13

Figure 13.   The loyalty model

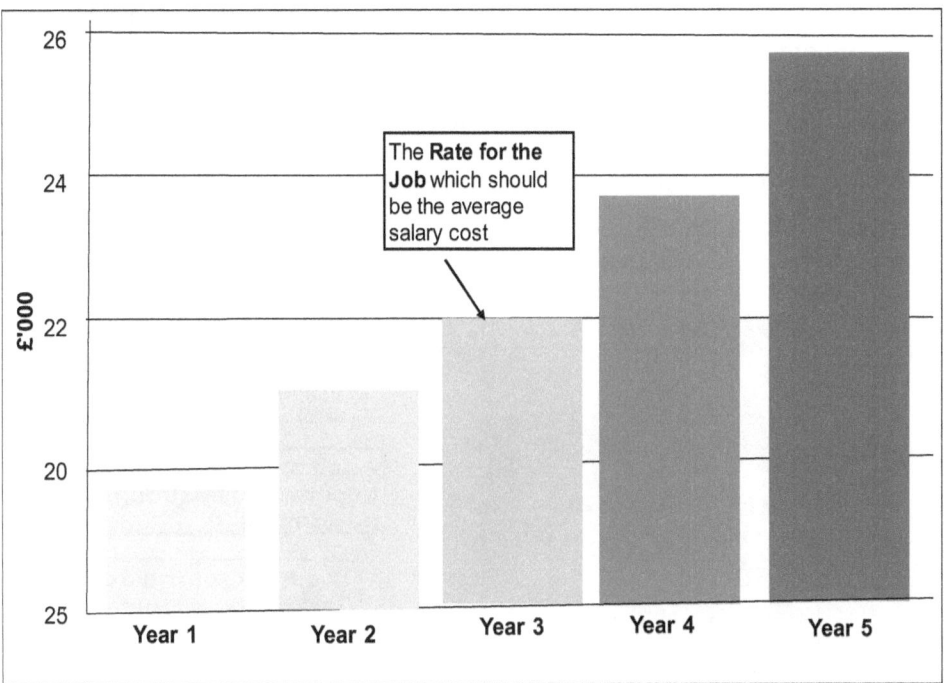

The strength of this model is that the pay structure is designed to purchase loyalty. Employees know that they may not be highly paid in the early part of their time in the role, but that if they stay with the employer for a number of years they will progress to a good level of salary. However, it is not an appropriate model for many modern jobs, but for some, especially in the public sector, it remains useful.

The last of the talent models is the **Contribution Model**. This is the model that should be applied where the capabilities of the jobholder have a significant impact on the results achieved in the job. Most senior management and professional jobs fall into this model.

Pay should be varied based on the contribution of the individual. The amount by which pay should vary depends on what would be a fair differential between a jobholder who is developing into the role, and the strongest possible performer in the same job. The variable amount of pay can be achieved in the form of additional base salary, bonus, or **non-consolidated pay,** which can be paid monthly with the salary, but which may be withdrawn if performance declines in future years.

Figure 14.   The contribution model

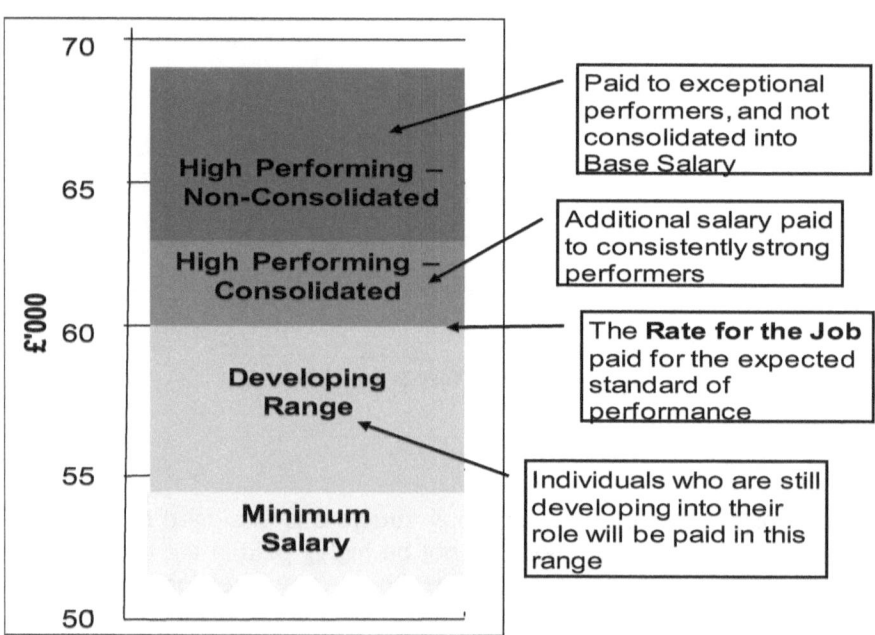

The illustration shows a rate for the job of £60,000. There is the potential to earn a further 15% of salary based on performance, of which 5% of salary may be consolidated into salary and the rest may be withdrawn if performance subsequently declines. Below the rate for the job, there is a developing range of around 10% of base salary.

Chapter 6. Performance and reward

This chapter looks at the arrangements for connecting pay with performance. It especially deals with the difficult area of individual performance and the performance management processes that are designed to support this. Reward can be formally connected to performance by varying the amount of salary, by using bonus or with non-consolidated pay.

The first step should be to define the objectives for linking performance and reward. One objective, which will be the Finance Director's priority, is to vary costs with business performance, so the business only pays out what it can afford. This should always be an overriding objective.

In the employment relationship, there is a hierarchy of possible objectives to consider. Performance-related pay can be used to:

1. Reflect market practice and to recruit and retain employees.
2. Communicate business priorities and share in success.
3. Reward employees fairly based on their individual contribution.
4. Create an incentive for improved performance.

These objectives are progressively more difficult to achieve. The first objective is relatively simple, but it is very difficult to achieve the final objective and use reward as an incentive.

If the objective is to reflect market practice, the overriding priority is to ensure that the amounts are competitive to enable the recruitment and retention of employees, although bonuses may also be linked to business and individual performance. This is the approach used in much of the financial services sector, where bonuses have to be paid to prevent employees moving to get larger bonuses at competitors. For jobs where the payment of bonuses is widespread, this is a necessary objective, although employers do not usually like to admit that they are paying bonuses for this reason.

The second objective is to use bonuses to communicate business priorities, to engage employees with the issues that are important to the business, and simultaneously to ensure that no payment is made unless business goals are achieved. Most employee profit sharing arrangements are designed for this purpose. Although often described as incentives, such arrangements work best as a means of engaging with employees and of connecting the cost of pay to the performance of the business. The objective is also important for team bonuses. If a team needs to work together to achieve a common purpose, linking reward to success can play an important role in engaging employees with what they need to do together to succeed.

The third objective, to reward employees fairly, is the most important for the digital age. For jobs where the capability of the individual employee has a large impact on the outputs that are achieved, this should be reflected in the way that the employee is rewarded. A pay system that fails to recognise significant differences in individual contributions is unfair and can easily become a psychological threat. For example, if x and y are doing the same job and x is making a bigger contribution than y, then x is likely to become demotivated if he/she is paid at the same level as y. This principle only applies for those types of jobs where the capabilities of the individual employee have a significant impact on the outputs of the job, and in the digital age, an increasing number of jobs are like this. The pay framework should be based on the Contribution Model that was discussed in Chapter 5.

The last and most difficult objective is to use performance-related pay as an incentive. Pay only works as an incentive for jobs that are comprised of simple repetitive tasks, which can easily be measured and linked to financial reward. For example, in a job that gives an employee the task of making 200 units in a week, it may be possible to design an incentive to make 220 units a week if the there is scope for the task to be carried out more productively. This can work if the employee is aware of how he is doing against the target and can clearly see how much more has to be done in order to receive more pay for the week. Most modern jobs are too complex for activities and results to be measured in this way. Usually the quality of the work and the customer experience are as important as the outputs achieved and it is more difficult to measure these.

Most bonus schemes claim to be designed to achieve all four of these objectives simultaneously. However, this claim sends ambiguous messages to employees, adds to the complexity of bonus scheme design, and creates the threat of uncertainty. Employers should decide which of the four objectives is most important for the business and design and communicate the bonus to fit with that objective. If it is not possible to design a bonus scheme that can be explained to employees, it is better not to use bonuses at all.

The remainder of this chapter deals with the formal arrangements for linking pay with performance. Employers can also use recognition schemes to reward exceptional contribution from individuals and teams, and sometimes the rewards can take the form of gifts rather than cash. These less formal arrangements can be a valuable part of reward if they are managed well, as small interventions can have a big impact.

In the digital age, the main challenge in reward management is in finding ways to formally connect pay with individual performance to achieve the third objective. This depends on having in place the processes and capabilities to measure individual performance.

Performance management

As jobs become more complex and flexible, it is not possible to have a fair pay system unless it recognises the contribution individual employees make. This raises the difficult question as to how performance should be measured, which is usually done through what is commonly called a performance management process. The performance management process usually attempts to rate individual performance, and it is these ratings that are commonly linked to pay.

The way performance management operates in most organisations does nothing to engage employees. The psychology of the rating (or box marking) system simply does not work. Most people think they are doing a better job than they actually are, and will be disappointed with the rating they get. Employees who are disappointed with their rating perceive a threat to their status, with all the psychological damage that goes with this. The negative impact on an employee, who receives a low rating, even if they were expecting it, will be proportionately greater than the positive impact on those who receive higher ratings. The performance management process also creates the threat of uncertainty as the dreaded annual appraisal round draws closer.

Organisations usually assess whether their performance management process is working by looking at whether objectives are set and annual appraisals are carried out on a timely basis. They invest in IT systems to measure if these things are done, and once the system is in place everything seems easy to measure and data on individual performance is available. Organisations can easily fall into the trap of thinking they are managing performance when all they are actually doing is managing a process. Seldom do employers look at the important questions:

- What is the impact of the performance management process on employees?
- Is performance management actually achieving the objectives we set for it?

Performance management processes make the mistake of treating employees as if they are clocks. It is sometimes possible to set so called SMART[15] objectives at the start of the year, monitor progress towards those objectives during the year, and then to come up with an assessment of the extent to which the objectives are achieved. However, in reality it rarely works out like this because objectives change as business priorities change during year.

What is almost impossible is to assess is what the individual contribution towards the achievement of the objective is. Objectives are too complex and dependent on factors that are beyond the control of the individual to enable this to be done. It is possible to measure the skills and effort that employees bring to the task, and to assess performance on that basis, but there can be uncertainty about the relationship between that effort and the results achieved. Performance management processes do not recognise the role that luck plays in most business activity. Once employees understand the process they will make sure they have evidence to show what they have achieved, and that this was due to their efforts rather than luck. The annual appraisal often ends up being a negotiation that does real damage to the employment relationship.

Employers try to measure performance through a performance management process because business overvalues things that can be measured. "What gets measured gets done" is the cliché that is often used[16]. This may be true, but it is only a small part of the truth - many things are done that are not, and never could be measured. Often these are the most important things: providing great service to a customer, coming up with a creative innovation in the design of a product, working to help your colleagues out of a difficulty, or working unnoticed late one evening to meet a deadline.

In the world of accountants and management consultants, who are paid to measure things, everything is treated like a clock. They see clouds as too "fluffy", too unpredictable, and too difficult to understand. Therefore, they try to turn them into clocks or ignore them. Some readers of this book might be dismissive of the concept of intrinsic reward precisely because it cannot be measured. The problem is that we are blind to things we cannot see, and these are usually the things that cannot be measured. This problem is made worse in the business world by trying measure things that simply cannot be measured. Accountants are especially susceptible to the delusion that they understand things just because they count them.

It might be equally true to say "What gets measured does not work". The very act of setting a target can discredit the target and do harm to the organisation[17]. There are many examples of this: it is common practice for the timing of when sales are closed to be manipulated to fit with sales targets, and on a larger scale, companies will work to ensure that their annual results are in line with expectations. When doctors were rewarded based on the time it takes to get an appointment, it became impossible to book an appointment more than two days in advance to ensure that the target was met. In call centres, it is possible to measure most things, and this is why we all have bad experiences with them. The relentless pursuit of targets was why Mid Staffordshire NHS Trust forgot that it was supposed to be caring for patients, with terrible consequences resulting from this failure. The use of targets in schools remains controversial – should the performance of a school be based on academic attainment, at the expense of other less measurable criteria?

Setting a target is like moving from the rational world of Newtonian physics into the strange world of quantum mechanics, where it is impossible to know with certainty where things are or whether they exist at all. This not to say that targets should not be used and that things should not be measured. The point is that all targets should be treated with care and suspicion, and this is especially the case if they are linked to individual performance and reward.

Businesses like to use targets for two reasons: firstly, it is easy to set targets in a digital age with so much data available. The second reason is that managers like to set targets because they feel it gives them control. For employees control is a threat to their autonomy and it compromises intrinsic motivation. Our brains have evolved to do anything we can to overcome a threat and the target setters, with their spreadsheets, scorecards and performance metrics, do not usually understand that they may be doing more harm than good. It is because targets are a threat that they so often lead to unethical behaviour.

The obsession with trying to measure things means that employers give a lot of attention to the distribution of performance ratings. They worry about whether these are consistent across different parts of the organisation, and what the distribution is telling them about the performance of the workforce. There is often a rather sterile debate about how many employees fall into each ratings category, and sometimes this leads to the futile discussion about whether the system would be improved with either 4, 5, or 6 different categories. This is about how performance should be measured and has nothing to do with actual performance.

For large employers the typical process for determining performance ratings requires an initial assessment to be made by a line manager. There is then a "moderation meeting" with the next level of management, which the line manager may not even attend. In this meeting, senior managers will try to make an objective and fair decision on the relative merits of the performance of around 50 individuals over the performance year. With limited time, they will try to assess the individual performance for these employees over a total of around 11,000 working days. Even if they managed to get this right based on the information available in the meeting, the process does not add anything of value.

Performance management processes give senior people the illusion that they are managing people, when they are really just taking part in a process. The availability heuristic means that they will overestimate the significance of what they know, and become blind to anything they do not know. In the business world, this problem is exacerbated, because those who are confident in what they know (and have been lucky with this) get to senior positions.

The strange need for a performance management process and ratings comes from the fact that our brains are programmed to try to measure and look for patterns in things. We also disregard information that is not readily available to us. For example, employees who have sorted out known problems will be recognised, but those who may have contributed far more by preventing problems from occurring in the first place are usually overlooked. There are good psychological reasons why it is almost impossible to get an accurate picture of individual performance through the performance management process.

Employers also like to identify the high flyers, which the business should support and fast track for promotion. It is difficult enough to assess past performance accurately and fairly through the performance management processes - making fair assessments of future performance and potential is almost impossible. Employers do this because they think they are managing talent, which is important. However, what they are really doing is managing yet another process to put people into categories, trying to develop patterns and structures for something that is inherently unmeasurable.

If the employer decides that they wish to be "open and transparent" about the talent management process and to tell employees about their future potential this will have perverse results. Employees who are not identified as high flyers will, of course, see this as a threat. However, those who are told they are high flyers often become complacent, and they may not develop as quickly as they would without this information. Some value comes from this process because of the sharing of information about individuals and the discussion which flows from that. However, it can only be a valuable exercise in identifying talent if senior managers also recognise that they will often get it wrong.

The purposes of performance management and talent management processes are often unclear. Are they to:

1. Manage performance, and in particular to address areas of poor performance?

2. To support the development of people and improve performance?

3. Provide management with a metric that measures performance, and supports the management of pay increases and bonuses?

4. Identify talent and support talent management?

5. Enable a connection between performance and reward?

Most performance management systems purport to do all of these things, and the emphasis on each of the five purposes varies from one organisation to another.

The reality of individual performance is that there is usually a small minority of employees where pro-active performance improvement measures need to be put in place. If these do not work within a reasonable time, the employee should leave the organisation. However, the vast majority of employees are doing the jobs they are paid to do and do not need a performance management process. They need support and development through coaching and training. The process of performance management, especially if it includes performance ratings, is likely to do more harm than good.

Individual performance-related pay

Linking individual performance to pay is controversial because most people approach the issue based on their personal experiences, and the prejudices that come from these. In the public sector, they tend to believe that performance-related pay is "divisive" and contrary to the "public sector ethos"; conversely many private sector business leaders assume, as a matter of principle, that having performance-related pay is essential to business performance. These polarised attitudes are not very helpful: organisations are simply too complex and diverse to be susceptible to general principles and dogma. The right approach can only be developed by understanding the context for each organisation.

Many employers would like to get rid of their performance management systems, knowing that they add no practical value. The process of using performance ratings across the whole workforce and placing all employees into categories makes no sense, unless it is necessary to do this to manage reward. It is for this reason that many employers feel they need to keep their performance management processes in place. The questions to ask are: is it possible to get rid of performance management systems and to retain the concept of linking pay with individual performance? Should pay be linked to individual performance at all?

The first thing to establish is whether the job is suitable for individual performance-related pay. Employers often design systems of individual performance-related pay and apply them to all the talent models and jobs in the organisation on the same basis. This does not work for the simple reason that some jobs are much better suited to individual performance-related pay than others.

Based on the nature of the job two tests should be applied:

- **The Differentiation test:** is the job such that individuals are likely to contribute at different levels?

- **The Measurability test:** is it possible to measure the differences in individual contribution?

The first of these tests is relatively straightforward and widely accepted. Larger bonuses tend to be paid for managerial and professional jobs where individual capabilities have a significant impact on business performance. These are jobs which fall into the contribution model outlined in Chapter 5.

It is the second of the tests that is more often overlooked. If the first test is passed, the assumption is made that performance can be measured. It is assumed that the problem can be dealt with by stronger performance management processes, and by training to improve management capability. This may be part of the solution, but it is always more difficult to measure performance in some types of jobs than others. The quadrant model below summarises how the two tests should be considered, and gives examples of the types of jobs typically falling into each section:

Figure 15.   Applying the differentiation and measurability tests

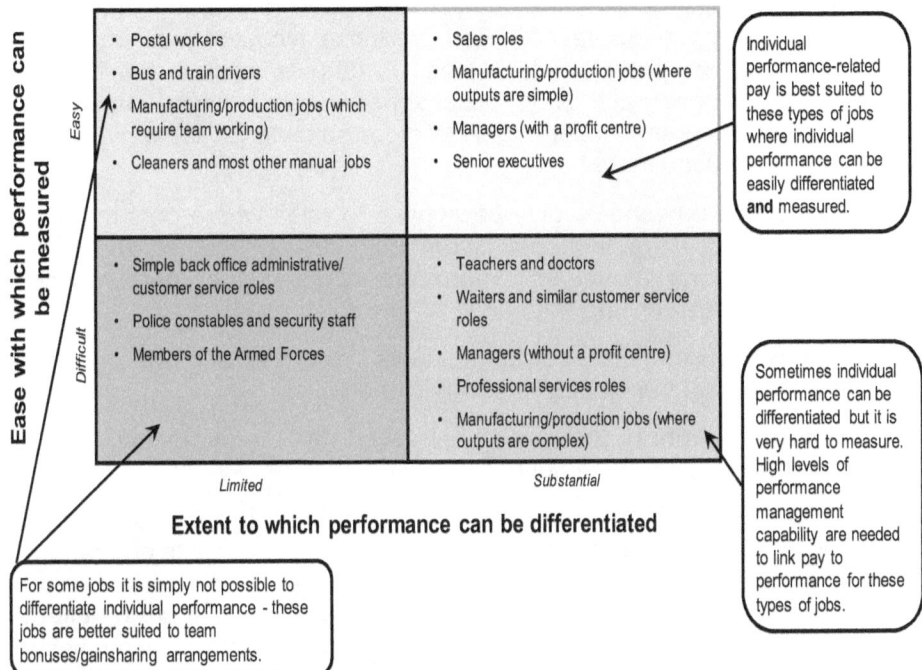

Ease with which performance can be measured

Easy

- Postal workers
- Bus and train drivers
- Manufacturing/production jobs (which require team working)
- Cleaners and most other manual jobs

- Sales roles
- Manufacturing/production jobs (where outputs are simple)
- Managers (with a profit centre)
- Senior executives

Individual performance-related pay is best suited to these types of jobs where individual performance can be easily differentiated **and** measured.

Difficult

- Simple back office administrative/ customer service roles
- Police constables and security staff
- Members of the Armed Forces

- Teachers and doctors
- Waiters and similar customer service roles
- Managers (without a profit centre)
- Professional services roles
- Manufacturing/production jobs (where outputs are complex)

Sometimes individual performance can be differentiated but it is very hard to measure. High levels of performance management capability are needed to link pay to performance for these types of jobs.

Limited   *Substantial*

Extent to which performance can be differentiated

For some jobs it is simply not possible to differentiate individual performance - these jobs are better suited to team bonuses/gainsharing arrangements.

For jobs in the top right quadrant, individual performance-related pay is appropriate and these jobs fit into the contribution model.

In the top left quadrant, individual performance-related pay is unlikely to work: although the measurability test is passed individuals cannot, on their own, increase outputs without adding to their working hours or compromising on risk and/or quality. For these jobs the market or the retention models are most likely to be appropriate, although in some instances the career model could be used.

The bottom right quadrant is the danger area. These are jobs where it is clear that performance can be differentiated, but it is very difficult to measure performance. They are jobs where the outputs depend on how the expertise and knowledge of the jobholder is used, and this is determined by the professional expertise of the jobholder. The work tends to be self-directed and there is no easy way of quantify the outputs. It is very likely to do more harm than good if **output measures** are used for these types of jobs because targets often lead to perverse outcomes. If outputs cannot readily be measured the best approach is to assess performance based on **input measures**, and the career model might be more suitable for these types of jobs than the contribution model.

Performance-related pay should only be applied to roles where performance can be differentiated. It is then necessary to consider whether and how performance should be measured. There are two types of performance measures that could be considered:

1. **Input measures:** the knowledge, skills, competencies, values and behaviours that the employee brings to the job.

2. **Output measures:** the results achieved by the individual which normally form part of the annual objectives.

Most employers look at both output and input measures so they can take a rounded view of performance. Of the two types of measures, inputs are harder to measure so output measures tend to prevail. One alternative is to take a binary approach so that input measures are defined at a minimum required standard, and the individual does not receive any pay for performance unless this minimum standard is attained. This binary approach removes the need to make complex assessment of performance against input measures. It is a simple Yes/No decision. It is also helpful to have performance against input measures linked to base salary, with performance against output measures linked to bonus. This is because an individual's performance against input measures are less likely to fluctuate from one year to the next.

Any decision on individual performance must be based on a judgement. It is a fallacy that performance decisions can be "objective", in the sense that everything can be objectively measured. Ultimately, all decisions about people in an organisation require subjective judgements to be made: for example, decisions on hiring and promotions involve judgements about future performance and these are always subjective. Developing the capabilities to make those judgments rationally should be an essential part of reward management.

Is it necessary to have a performance management system, with all the difficulties of setting targets and objectives, and with the psychologically damaging rating system? For input measures, the performance management process is not necessary. The knowledge, skills and behaviours that are required should be defined as part of the job. Developmental processes (feedback, coaching, training etc.) should be in place to build the skills and competencies that are needed and to ensure that employees are equipped to adapt to changes as required.

Employees should have the opportunity to develop their skills if they wish to do so. For those who value this, it is part of their reward, both extrinsic and intrinsic. Reward should be linked to the development of skills and competencies, provided that additional reward for the additional capabilities is affordable. This may be achieved because a more highly skilled workforce can be more productive, or through the promotion of some employees to a more highly skilled job. Where employers are unable to reward additional skills because they are not affordable, they should be open about this. There should be no mismatch between expectations and reward.

The measurement of outputs is rather more difficult. It is only for jobs in the top right of the quadrant, where performance can be measured and differentiated, that output measures should be used in linking individual performance with pay. The crucial question is whether there are measurable outputs for which the job has responsibility. For executive and management jobs, there should be measureable outputs, as there should be for sales jobs.

It is also much better to talk about pay being linked to the outputs from the job, rather than being described as an incentive. The point is that pay should vary with the outputs achieved to be fair to both the employee and the employer, and should be linked to the degree of effort and skill that the employee brings in contributing to these outputs. This means that employees will not be personally threatened if the desired outputs are not achieved through no fault of their own, and they will be less likely to "game" the targets.

The absence of output measures for some jobs will not make the Finance Director happy. He (because it usually is a he) will want to be sure that the costs of pay vary with profitability. The answer to this problem is in managing expectations and engaging with employees on issues relating to the performance of the business. Employees need to understand that increases in pay must be affordable. Performance-related pay often goes wrong when employees are told that their individual efforts will be rewarded (or incentivised!), and subsequently discover that they will not be paid what they are expecting because the business is not doing well enough. If a bonus is less than the amount the employee believes she has earned, or worked for, she will have suffered a loss and a threat to the needs for status and fairness.

The flowchart in Figure 16 should be used as a guide to making decisions about individual performance-related pay:

Figure 16. **Deciding on individual performance-related pay**

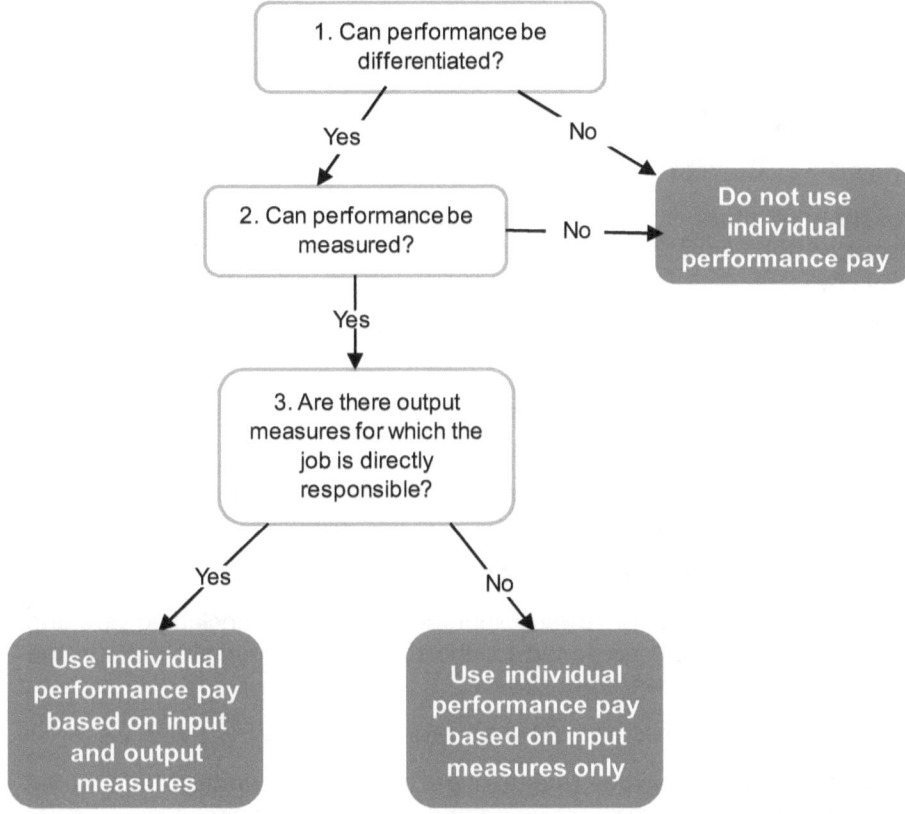

Chapter 7. Reward management

In this final chapter, we look at some of the practical issues in introducing a new pay framework and the different types of capabilities that are needed to manage reward in the digital age.

Introducing a new pay framework

The stages that should be followed in designing a pay framework are:

Stage 1.   Current State Analysis

Ensure that there is a full understanding of how reward is currently managed and how it fits with the needs of the business. The best way to do this is by:

- A comprehensive analysis of data on the operation of the current arrangements.

- Talking with managers and employees to get their perspective on how the current approach operates.

- Using these discussions to understand the role of reward in engaging employees, including both extrinsic and intrinsic reward.

Stage 2.   Design Pay Framework

Identify what the optimal reward approach should be, including how the pay framework should be varied for the different segments of jobs in the workforce. The pay framework should:

- Support the business and HR strategies.

- Be easily communicated to employees so they can understand it in the context of the work they are doing and their career aspirations.

- Provide a fair and affordable level extrinsic reward and support intrinsic reward.

Stage 3.   Develop Business Case

Show the costs and benefits of changes, and especially identify how they will support HR and business strategies. The business case should include the plan to move towards the recommended approach, including prioritisation and the phased implementation of changes.

Stage 4.   Implement

Use the Business Case as the basis for implementation, ensuring that there is a clear and consistent message as to why the changes need to be made.

Changes to pay frameworks involve uncertainty, which is one of the psychological threats. This is unavoidable. However much people might dislike the current reward arrangements, they are likely to dislike the idea of change even more. The best time to make a change to a pay framework is when other changes are happening in the business, and the new framework is needed to support those other changes. Any organisation changes are good opportunities to make changes to pay frameworks. In these circumstances, the business case for making changes to pay can be based on the business case as to why the wider changes are needed.

When introducing a pay framework, you will need to overcome the psychological biases described in Chapter 2. For example, people will base their thinking on what has grabbed their attention rather than seeing the big picture, and will look for easy answers in data and processes. Here are a few tips, which may be helpful:

- If you have agreed some anodyne principles do not think you have made progress. Identify the implications of the principles so that everyone understands exactly is being agreed.

- Be very careful with market pay benchmarking and, if possible, do not rely on a single source of market data. Use the data to inform the design of the pay framework, but do not attach too much importance to the precise market positioning of pay.

- Find out what people think they want, but also be prepared to challenge them. If someone thinks he/she knows what the right solution should be, it is very likely to be based on something they think they have seen work in the past. It may not be the right answer for your organisation.

- Do not get bogged down with transitional issues until the overall direction of travel is sorted out. Get agreement on what the optimal pay framework should look like, and then sort out how to do the transition. If the transition is difficult, it will take time to get there, but you can still take positive steps in the right direction.

Enhancing the reward function

In most organisations, there is much room for improvement in the way reward is managed and communicated. This requires an enhanced role for the reward function and an upskilling of reward professionals. HR functions usually suffer from being dominated by finance, and finance professionals sometimes have difficulties in dealing with anything that does not have numbers attached to it. Reward functions tend to be made up of people who like numbers and communicate with the finance people. This is why reward is often unconnected with HR and talent management. Much of reward management is about managing costs, the annual pay review process and negotiating within the organisation on what is the correct market rate for a particular job. Very little attention is given to making reward a part of the employment relationship.

Most HR people avoid reward, viewing it as a difficult technical function, which is best left alone. Reward professionals are usually quite analytical. They understand the legal and technical aspects of reward and are on top the numbers, but they often have limited understanding of how reward should connect with HR and talent management. Reward specialists often spend most of their time and resources on executive remuneration (looking after the important people!) and only turn their attention to the wider workforce during the annual pay review process.

Pay and reward gets very little management attention, although it is often a substantial cost for the employer. Companies usually have large teams to manage other costs, such as estates, tax or purchasing and procurement. This might be because pay seems relatively straightforward, but it might also be because it is safest to leave it alone and not to change it very much. This can be complacent, because the consequences of getting it wrong are considerable. Poor management of pay can easily lead to costs getting out control, and mistakes in the way it is communicated can have a huge negative impact on employees.

Reward should be a central part of the employment relationship. If it is managed well it will strengthen the relationship, and it is the role of the reward professional to make that happen. This requires an enhancement and shift in emphasis in the skills that are needed. Reward professionals need to understand how reward fits with the wider employment relationship, and the behavioural science of reward. Reward also needs to be better integrated with the rest of HR and throughout the business. The ultimate goal of reward specialists should be that everyone in the business understands why they are paid as they are, and has realistic expectations of what they will be paid in the future.

Thunder Cloud – Managing Reward in a Digital Age

The basic skills that are typically found in a reward function, together with the additional skills that are needed for the digital age, are set out below:

Basic	Additional
Skills and competencies: • Analytical skills and data analysis • Project management Knowledge: • Market pay data • Job evaluation/sizing/levelling • Legal aspects of reward and terms and conditions • Share incentives • Pensions and benefits • Reward information systems	Skills and competencies: • Relationship building • Presentation skills • Seeing the "big picture" as to how reward fits with HR and business strategy Knowledge: • Performance management • Training and development • Succession planning • Psychology/behavioural economics

Conclusion

Thunder Cloud – Managing Reward in a Digital Age

Reward management is being bamboozled by the digital age. Some employers still cling to the Roman army model and others rely on the dubious concept that there is a "market" for pay. Many are stuck somewhere between these two alternative and do not know where to look for answers. Much of the answer lies in using behavioural science to find new ways of managing reward and the employment relationship.

Reward is not like a clock - it is like a dark and unpredictable cloud. It is part of a complex ecosystem where the effect of changes cannot be predicted – very small changes can have a big impact, whether negative or positive. Reward can only make a positive contribution if it supports the employment relationship and supports the psychological needs of employees. If it does not do this, it becomes a threat, and can have a severe negative impact.

For employees with a real career path, reward should be designed to fit with progression through that career. Where they are in a job that requires skills that can readily be transferred to other employers it should be treated as a market-facing role, and reward should be competitive with that of other employers. However, there is little value in designing career paths for market facing roles, and market alignment is less important for jobs where there is a real career path. Pay frameworks should be connected with the talent models within which employees operate.

Pay should only be linked to performance if there is a clear basis for doing this. Performance-related pay should not normally be used as an incentive, but it can play a vital role in engaging employees with what the organisation is trying to achieve and sharing in its success. For jobs where individual contribution makes a real difference to the outcome, pay may be unfair if it is not connected with individual performance. For these types of jobs, individual performance pay may be needed to prevent a threat to the strongest performers.

Any uncertainty, or failure to meet expectations, also means that reward becomes a threat to employees. This is likely to provoke a strong and irrational response. The human brain has evolved to respond to threats quickly and spontaneously, and threats can only be negated by paying fairly, managing expectations, and communicating well.

Increasing the level of pay is unlikely to work in the long term. Reward is addictive, and the main impact of pay increases may be to raise expectations for the next time. Employers who do this soon lose control of costs and have unhappy employees.

Reward should no longer be a technical analytic function that is best left alone to do its own thing. Pay is a substantial cost for many businesses and, if it is managed well, it can be used to support what the business is doing to manage talent. If it is managed poorly, it can prevent the whole organisation from succeeding.

Here are some final tips for managing reward in the digital age:

- Put as much effort into managing employee expectations as into deciding on the amount of reward.

- Remember that the negative impact of getting it wrong is always going to be greater than the positive impact of getting it right.

- Do whatever you can to ensure that reward is consistent with what the business is doing to manage talent.

- Do not link pay to performance unless you have a valid reason for doing this.

- Do not rely on data, processes and systems to tell you what to do.

- Never forget that reward is central to the employment relationship.

Like a thunder cloud, reward can be dark and menacing but it is also good fun, endlessly fascinating and bright sunshine is never too far behind. If you invest in relationships, understand the behavioural aspects of reward, and are ready to be surprised, you will make a valuable contribution by managing reward well. And you will certainly have some fun along way!

Definitions

One of the problems with reward, and with human resources more generally, is the incoherence and inconsistency in the language that is so often used. Words can very easily take on a meaning that was not intended. One of the objectives of this book is to bring a new and useful vocabulary to reward management.

These are some of the key terms used in this book, together with the meaning that is intended:

Career Model	The talent management and reward model that is based on a career, with movement upwards from one job to the next.
Career Path	A structure that involves progression to a more senior role within the same specialist area or profession.
Contribution Model	The talent management and reward model for jobs where variations in individual contribution can make a significant difference to the outputs from the job.
Differentiation test	The test as to whether the nature of the job is such that

	individuals are likely to contribute at different levels.
Crowding out	Where extrinsic reward, such as pay, comes to dominate so that the value of intrinsic reward is lost.
Employment relationship	This refers to the relationship between the employer and the employee. Reward is part of that relationship as are all other aspects of what is commonly called the Employment Value Proposition.
Extrinsic reward	Reward that comes to the employee externally, such as pay, pension, benefits and share incentives.
Input measures	The knowledge, skills, competencies and behaviours that the employee brings to the job.
Intrinsic reward	Reward that comes internally by meeting the psychological needs of the individual.
Job Evaluation	A formal analytic process to measure the size of a job. It assesses the role in terms of the levels of knowledge and skills required, and the level of responsibility. Some job evaluation systems also look at other aspects of the job, such as the emotional or physical demands that are placed on the jobholder.
Job size	The size of the job measured by job evaluation or some other form of job sizing.
Market Model	The talent management and reward model in which pay needs to match the external market.
Market rate	The amount that is typically paid by other employers for the same job.

Measurability test	The test as to whether it is possible to measure the differences in individual contribution.
Non-consolidated	An element of cash pay that does not form part of base salary. This includes bonus and other elements of cash reward that do not from part of base salary.
Output measures	The results achieved by the individual which normally form part of the annual objectives.
Pay	This refers to cash pay such as salary and bonus. It does not include benefits or share incentives.
Pay framework	The system and processes through which pay decisions are made.
Performance	The amount paid for performance, which may be organisational, team or individual performance.
Rate for the job	The amount an organisation decides should be paid for a particular job. It should be informed by market data where this can be relied on, but also by job size.
Retention Model	The talent management and reward model that is designed to retain employees in the same job without movement through a career path.
Reward	Extrinsic rewards such as pay (salary and bonuses), pension, benefits and share incentives. In also includes the psychological, or intrinsic rewards, which are a vital part of employment relationships in the digital age.
Reward strategy	Employers should have an HR/People Strategy and in this book reward strategy is used to describe reward as part of this wider strategy. Although the phrase is

	commonly used, it is doubtful if there can be such a thing as a reward strategy which operates independently from the rest of HR.
Segment(ation)	In this book, this means segmenting the workforce by reference to the different types of jobs using the talent models. Sometimes the term is used to talk about segmentation by age or some other category.
Talent models	Models as to how talent is managed which can be used for reward design.

Some words to avoid

Words matter. Without a common vocabulary, ideas cannot easily be understood and are of little practical use. The HR world is littered with words that are misused and have no real meaning. Here are some words that are not helpful and which I have tried to avoid in this book.

Employment Value Proposition	This is sometimes used to describe the value that the employee receives from the employment relationship. In this book, the word reward is used instead – it is simpler and means the same thing!
Incentives	Incentives belong to the world of accountants and economists. Where it is used in reward management it is often misleading and a travesty of the true meaning of the word.
Job families	Job families are one of those HR fads and many organisations have spent vast amounts of resources in developing job families. Usually they do not know why they are doing this but because other organisations are "doing job families" it is on the list of things categorised as "best practice".
Pay structure	Pay framework is the used instead of pay structure. Structure implies a level of order and rigour that is usually unachievable in the management of reward.

Notes

---

[1] Karl Popper, Karl. *"Of Clouds and Clocks - An Objective Approach to the Problem of Rationality and the Freedom of Man"* The Arthur Holly Compton Memorial Lecture Presented at Washington University, 1965.

[2] Payscales chart for the Roman army – Hadrian's Wall Country at http://hadrianswallcountry.co.uk.

[3] Oxford English Dictionary definition.

[4] CIPD Research Report *"Show me the money! – The behavioural science of reward"*, 2015.

[5] Rock, David *"SCARF: a brain based model for collaborating with and influencing others"* NeuroLeadership Journal, 2008.

[6] There is now a huge body of evidence for systematic biases in academic research. For further reading on the subject I would recommend:

- Taleb, Nassim *"The Black Swan: The Impact of the Highly Improbable" Random House, 2007.*

- Kahneman, Daniel *"Thinking Fast, and Slow" - Farrar, Straus and Giroux, 2011.*

- Sunstein, Cass and Thaler, Richard, *"Nudge: Improving Decisions about Health, Wealth and Happiness", Yale University Press, 2008.*

[7] Summed up beautifully in Daniel Kahneman's book, Thinking Fast, and Slow: "Nothing in life is quite as important as you think it is when you are thinking about it."

[8] Extract from the NHS Agenda for Change Job Evaluation Handbook.

[9] Where a number of buyers are bidding for products in a market where supply is limited, the successful bidder will usually end up pay more than the product is worth. Thaler, Richard. *"Anomalies – The Winner's Curse" The Journal of Economic Perspectives, 1988.*

[10] An incentive is defined in the Oxford English Dictionary as "A thing that motivates or encourages someone to do something".

[11] Average CEO remuneration in the FTSE100 is £4.96 million and the average UK salary is £27,645 *High Pay Centre, March 2016.*

[12] Self-employment accounted for around one third of the growth in employment in the UK labour market in the period since 2010.

[13]. Pink, Daniel. *"Drive – The Surprising Truth About What Motivates Us" Riverhead Hardcover, 2009* has a good explanation of how extrinsic motivation crowds out intrinsic motivation.

[14] Nassim Taleb's book, The Black Swan, explains how this bias caused by "silent evidence". We see the people at the top and assume that they have got

there because they have exceptional talent. We underestimate the role of luck in career progression because we do not see all the other equally talented people who do not make it to the top because they did not have the same luck.

[15] SMART stands for Specific, Measurable, Attainable, Relevant and Time-bound and is the commonly used banality which is both a statement of the obvious and unattainable in the real world

[16] Attributed variously to Paul Drucker, Tom Peters etc.

[17] This is known as Goodhart's law after Charles Goodhart, the economist who developed it: "When a measure becomes a target, it ceases to be a good measure".